diary of a geisha girl

An Avon Original

AVON PUBLICATIONS, INC.
575 Madison Avenue • New York 22, N. Y.

I please my
first gentleman · · ·

I did not know quite what to expect
when the buzzer rang in my room that first
night and I was told a visitor would be
brought to my room.

I knew the art of the geisha—but the
men who came here were not like the ones
I had known.

I waited, silently hoping I could please
my first gentleman-san, for it would be a
good omen for success in this strange
new world.

There was a knock at the door . . .

KIMIKO OMURA
as told to
William Vaneer

———————————————

I SAW THE HOUSE FIRST on the evening of my arrival in the strange and beautiful islands of Hawaii. A thick growth of shrubbery and trees hid it from prying eyes along the old Pali road. The modern structure had a low-hanging green roof and large screened windows that looked out over a lovely tropical landscape in the lower Nuuanu Valley. It was designed so that each bedroom provided complete privacy and seclusion. It was a place of celestial serenity after the terror of my escape from assailants in Hakodate.

The sun was fading behind the Waiana Range as I stood with the Captain at the door. The air was quiet save for the liquid whistle of a mynah bird. Beyond a poinciana tree I glimpsed a patch of blue ocean on the far horizon. At that moment I wanted nothing more than to live in this secure place for the rest of my life. It was a strange feeling for a Japanese girl, born in the shadow of Fujiyama. I had never lived anywhere except in the great city of Tokyo where I grew up to become a geisha.

"We came to see Mrs. Reisner," said the Captain, when a Filipino man in a white dress jacket opened the door and looked out at us questioningly.

No doubt we were an odd pair. Captain Hagan wore slacks and a shirt and his sea cap was cocked to one side on his weatherbeaten head. I wore an oversized khaki shirt and a pair of men's trousers many times too large for me.

"May I ask who is calling?" said the man with cold politeness.

"Tell her Captain Hagan and be quick about it, lad. I phoned her this afternoon. She's expecting us," said the Captain.

The man disappeared but returned in a moment and showed us to a private office inside. A gray-haired woman sat with matronly ease behind a highly polished desk.

"Hello, Ev," said the Captain.

"How are you, Mert." The woman smiled. Then she saw me and her jaw dropped. "My God! What sort of a costume is that?"

"This is Kimiko Omura, the girl I told you about." He turned to me. "Meet Mrs. Evaline Reisner."

"Why are you dressed in that outfit?" she demanded. The Captain answered for me.

"The ship's store on that old tub of mine doesn't carry any women's clothes," he replied dryly.

Mrs. Reisner laughed. She told the Captain to go to the lanai and order a drink while she talked with me. When we were alone she looked me over from behind her desk. I grew self-conscious and embarrassed as I stood before her. She wagged her head.

"In all my years, this is the first time a girl has come to me for employment looking like some waif out of the gutter."

"It was the best we could do, Mrs. Reisner. The night I left Hakodate I looked even worse. Some friends passed me off to the Captain's ship as a boy. Otherwise, I might never have made it," I explained.

"Sit down," she said.

I looked around and saw a chair behind me. Her sharp eyes assessed me from my black hair to my

6

ankles, which showed below the rolled cuffs of my tattered trousers. I waited respectfully for her to speak.

"The Captain said you are experienced."

"I am a geisha."

"That means very little here. What has been your experience with men?"

"I have known many."

"Have you ever worked in a house?" she asked.

"In Tokyo I worked in a geisha house."

"There is a difference. It makes me wonder if you would be content here. I mentioned that to Captain Hagan when he called this afternoon," said Mrs. Reisner.

"So long as I have a chance to earn on my services, I will be quite content. That's really all I am seeking," I told her.

I knew the difference of which she spoke. It had been pointed out to me by friends in Tokyo. The Western world makes no distinction between a geisha and a pom-pom girl. I was prepared to accept that difference in my new life. There was no other choice open to me.

"How old are you, Kimiko?"

"Twenty-one."

"And where did you learn English?"

"From my aunt. She was a geisha herself and a highly cultured woman. It was she who raised me from a child after my parents were lost in a typhoon in the Tsugaru Strait. She taught me the geisha art and when I was old enough she obtained employment for me."

Mrs. Reisner sat back and lit a cigarette. I had riveted my attention on her the whole time we had been talking. Now I took a second glance around the office. It had panelled walls and thick carpeting. The furniture was modern Oriental and expensive.

"I can't tell much about your looks in a pair of men's trousers and shirt. Do you mind slipping them off?" she asked.

I was not accustomed to such an inspection but I had to find work. I unbuttoned my shirt and took it off, then dropped the trousers around my ankles and stepped out of them. I kept my head and shoulders proudly erect for I had nothing to be ashamed of.

"Hmmm," Mrs. Reisner mused. "Good shape and pretty legs. You're a bit taller than the average Japanese girl and that's all to the good. Very well."

"Do you approve of me?" I asked, pulling on my trousers a moment later.

"Yes."

"Then I am hired?" I was most anxious to know that, for I had only a few dollars to my name.

"Not yet. Tell me how you gained entry into United States territory. I can't have the authorities coming around to check up on you."

"But I have papers. They are all in order. My marriage to a Japanese-American was arranged in Hakodate. It was for the purpose of getting me here," I explained.

"I thought Captain Hagan smuggled you out." Mrs. Reisner looked at me sharply.

"He did. But that was only to escape Communist agents. As a geisha in Tokyo I learned some information for your country's agents and they gave me protection when the Communists made an attempt on my life."

"Where is your husband?"

"He was slain in Hakodate the night I was smuggled out. I hardly knew him and we were to be divorced here in your country. I lived in mortal fear for many weeks but that is all in the past now. I must make a new life," I said.

Mrs. Reisner sighed. "All right, Kimiko. I'll take you on. Your first month will be probationary. After that, if you're loyal and attentive to your work, you should enjoy a good future here."

8

"Thank you." Tears of gratitude filled my eyes as I bowed.

"There are a number of things we must attend to in the morning. A medical examination. Some clothes. And I'll want you to visit a photographer. I have a special arrangement about making appointments for my girls, but I'll explain that to you later. Tonight I want you to get a good rest."

Mrs. Reisner stood up. She summoned a Filipino girl who showed me to a room upstairs. The girl smiled as she told me that this is where I would live and work. Then she left me alone, pulling the door closed behind her.

I looked around the spacious bedroom. The walls were pale beige trimmed in white. Near the jalousie over the picture window were two easy chairs and a cocktail table. A dressing table, containing two gold shaded lamps, was centered on one wall and over it hung an enormous mirror. Across the room was a low, giant-sized bed.

After I had glanced into the tiled bathroom and admired the luxurious stall shower, I walked to one of the chairs and sat down. In my ridiculous clothing I must have looked as out of place in that room as a fisherman in the emperor's palace. I began to feel my first relaxation in weeks as I gazed through the jalousie at the far lights of Honolulu. In my heart was silent gratitude to the Fate that had brought me safely here.

Someday I hoped to return to my home island, when the incident that had involved me was forgotten. A pleasant drowsiness came over me. My worries were gone. I knew the art of the geisha for it had been my life's work, and I was not afraid that my ability would fail me in this new land. It was work, and nothing more, to a geisha.

Presently I arose and removed my shirt and trousers

9

and stretched out on the magnificent bed. I had only a few moments to realize how different this was from the bed rolls I had known all of my life, before I fell into a deep and peaceful slumber.

CHAPTER TWO

Early morning sunlight filled the room when I awoke. From long habit I was instantly alert. I sat up, stretched and rubbed my head. The room was still strange to me, but it was friendly. I was delighted to think that it was mine. I took a cool shower and rubbed myself vigorously with a towel. Refreshed, I started to get into my shirt and trousers when the Filipino girl came in.

"Mrs. Reisner wishes you to put this on, then join her for breakfast right away," she said, handing me a cotton print dress.

"Did I oversleep?" I was worried. It would be impolite to keep my new benefactor waiting.

"No. Mrs. Reisner is up early. She's going to take you into town."

I put on the dress. It was not the best fitting garment I had ever worn, but it was comfortable. The Filipino girl told me that her name was Lillian. I followed her downstairs and was shown to a dining room at the rear of the house.

Mrs. Reisner was sitting alone at the head of a table that was set for eight. The girls of the house were still asleep, for some of them had worked until dawn. At Mrs. Reisner's invitation I sat down. The man in the white coat came in and served me a juicy, golden pineapple fresh from the fields of Wahiawa. As we ate

11

breakfast, Mrs. Reisner explained what had to be done this morning.

"We'll get the medical examination out of the way first, then get you some clothes. I made an appointment for you at Johnny Takoga's for one o'clock."

"Who is he?" I asked.

"The photographer. I haven't explained yet how we work. We never have a congregation of girls in the parlor. Visitors are received individually in the rooms. If a gentleman wishes to make a selection, I show him each girl in her own photographic album. It prevents embarrassment on the part of the guest."

How different this was from the tea houses, yet both ways enjoyed quiet formality. Instead of listening to my music or my conversation, the gentleman-san would observe a picture of me. I did not let Mrs. Reisner see my amusement.

She warned me against any unnecessary noise or commotion. Most girls developed steady clients, she said. Each was to be entertained with the utmost refinement. The girls might drink with their guests in their rooms, but only with all night visitors. Even then, if a girl showed the slightest trace of losing her self-control she was immediately dismissed in disgrace.

"I might run a house, but no one can ever say I don't run it on a high level," Mrs. Reisner declared emphatically.

After breakfast we drove into Honolulu in a big, roomy American car. I was impressed by the clean new buildings and the vistas along the busy streets of the famed Pacific city. Americans, Japanese, Chinese and many other races crowded the sidewalks. People were smiling. No one seemed to be lonely. It gave me a feeling of friendly warmth.

We spent an hour in a doctor's office. After the examination he pronounced me in good health. The next stop

12

was a department store on Fort Street. I was amazed at the endless articles there were to buy. Around the corner on King was a shoe store which we visited. I was given a most ample supply of clothing and shoes. When the boxes were loaded in the trunk of the car, Mrs. Reisner headed for Waikiki.

"This is where you get the real treatment," she smiled.

I looked at her questioningly, but she did not enlighten me. Instead she pointed out the Iolani Palace, the statue of Kamehameha, united Hawaii's first king, and Diamond Head in the distance. Presently I received my first glimpse of the beach at Waikiki, of the Royal Hawaiian Hotel, of the Surf Rider and the Moana. Suddenly we turned off of Kalakaua Avenue and stopped before a small dress shop.

Inside I was introduced to a slender, middle-aged woman whom Mrs. Reisner referred to as "Sadie."

"What's your opinion of her, Sadie?" Mrs. Reisner asked, nodding toward me as I stared wide-eyed around the shop at the gorgeous dresses and lingerie.

Sadie studied me critically for a minute. Her voice was brisk and confident when she spoke.

"Devastatingly feminine, like most Japanese girls, but not quite so short as most. The boys will go for that build."

"Don't you think I know that?" Mrs. Reisner bantered.

"Keep her just a little Americanized. She'll be terrific in a cocktail dress. Black undies, of course. And I'd suggest a negligee that's black and sheer enough to see through. Her ivory skin is a natural for that. She'll need a kimono and a gold brocade obi for those who want a geisha."

I looked around at the mention of geisha. Mrs. Reisner saw me and laughed. She glanced at Sadie.

"Kimiko is a geisha. A real one."

13

"Really?" Sadie looked at me peculiarly.

"Okay. Get going. We only have until noon," said Mrs. Reisner.

Sadie swung into action. A seamstress was summoned from the back of the shop. I was draped, measured, pinned up and sized. A clerk stood by removing dresses from long glass-panelled cabinets as a dozen different garments were tried on me. I began to feel like a window mannikin in the stores along the Ginza.

Finally Mrs. Reisner and Sadie agreed on one evening dress, a cocktail dress, a kimono, two negligees, bras and panties and a supply of the sheerest, long smoky stockings I had ever seen. The evening dress required some alterations and would be delivered in the morning. The other clothes were put in boxes and carried out to the car.

On the way in from Waikiki we stopped for sandwiches at a restaurant overlooking the Ala Wai Canal. I had been wondering if Mrs. Reisner expected me to pay for the clothes and asked her about it as we ate.

"It's partly my investment in you, but since the clothes will be yours I'll deduct half the expense from your first month's earnings. After that it's up to you to maintain your wardrobe. I'll remind you if I think you're letting it slip," she said.

"Will I be permitted to buy something of my own?"

"Naturally. You can buy whatever you choose with your own money. But you won't need much. Some shorts and an aloha shirt or two to wear in the daytime and a couple of cotton dresses are about all any of the girls need."

"I won't be spending much. I hope to save my money," I told her.

"You'll be smart if you do," Mrs. Reisner said laconically.

Downtown again, she parked the car and had me

remove several boxes from the trunk. We went to a second-floor photographic studio and I met Johnny Takoga. He was a young nisei who made no attempt to hide his curious scrutiny of me.

"Do you think she'll photograph?" asked Mrs. Reisner.

"In spades," Johnny grinned.

"Make up the usual album. When can you have it ready?"

"Tomorrow."

Mrs. Reisner had some business at the bank. Johnny would need two hours for his work. She told me that she would pick me up here at the studio.

"Meanwhile, pose for him the way he says. He's a cheesecake specialist," said Mrs. Reisner and departed.

"What is a cheesecake specialist?" I asked. I had heard Americans in Tokyo use the expression, but I had never been told what it meant.

"Pictures of girls, especially their legs and knockers. Sexy stuff, like you've got plenty of, sweetheart."

My cheeks grew warm. I did not like this Johnny Takoga. He was too impudent and shameless. He removed the clothes from the boxes and looked at them. He turned to me and winked.

"That old gal really knows what entices men. Well, let's get at it. The cocktail gown first. Later, you might get too warm for it under the lights."

I changed into the cocktail dress. At Johnny's request I pulled on a pair of dark stockings and got into my high-heeled shoes. I spent the next twenty minutes in the glare of two blazing lights, smiling and posturing at his direction, and disliking him more all the time. But I was working for Mrs. Reisner, not him. If this was her wish, I would not complain.

"Have you ever done any modelling?" he asked.

"No."

15

"You should. You're quite a dish."

"I'm a geisha," I snapped.

"There's a different name for that in Honolulu," he laughed.

He took full-length shots of me, head and shoulder shots, face on and profile. He had me remove the cocktail dress and pose in the black undies and long stockings. I was photographed standing and kneeling and sitting on a table hugging my knees. Finally he made me stand before the camera naked.

"That wraps it up," he said two hours later.

I was thankful that it was over. It had been an ordeal because of the way he had looked at me the whole time. He stood aside as I put on my street dress, then offered me a cigarette which I refused.

"You didn't come out from the mainland, did you?" he asked.

"No."

"Funny, I haven't seen you around here before."

"I came from Japan, only yesterday."

"Let me know if you ever want to pick up some extra change modelling, but don't say anything about it to Mrs. Reisner."

"I have no intention of doing something against her wish," I said curtly.

"It's your body, toots," he smiled.

It was late afternoon when Mrs. Reisner and I returned to the house. We carried the boxes inside. Two girls, who had been sunbathing on the lanai, came in at that moment and I was introduced to Betty Richards, a small blonde, and Vanessa Drake, a redhead. They helped carry the boxes to my room.

As Betty Richards was about to leave, I asked her what time dinner was served.

"Six o'clock, and don't be late," she advised.

I spent the next half-hour putting away my wardrobe.

After that I took a shower, groomed myself with care and went downstairs. It was not quite six, but two girls were already at the table. One was a large blonde and the other was a brown-skinned girl.

"You must be the new one," said the blonde.

"That's right. I am Kimiko Omura," I replied, smiling pleasantly.

"My name is Helen Gray and this is Lemomie," said the blonde. "Glad to have you aboard."

But neither Helen's voice nor her frosty eyes seemed to bear out the meaning of her words. Betty Richards arrived at the table in a moment. Five minutes later Mrs. Reisner came in with Vanessa. They had already begun to eat when a French girl came in and I was introduced to Colette.

"Now you've met everyone except Dolores who's spending a few days' vacation on the big island," said Mrs. Reisner.

The girls talked during dinner and I listened closely, hoping to learn more of this new life. But their talk was about the motion pictures and clothes and holidays, which contributed little to my knowledge.

After dinner Mrs. Reisner went to her office. The girls wandered back to their rooms. I remained at the table at Helen's suggestion. We were alone except for Colette who was finishing her ice cream.

"I take it you're no beginner at this," Helen remarked.

"I am a geisha," I said.

Helen gave me a hard smile. "We all get along fine and the reason we do is that we don't go after each other's customers."

I looked at the girl with surprise. I had no intention of stealing anyone's customers. Helen cocked her head at Colette.

"Isn't that right, Frenchie?"

The girl nodded.

"Just you remember that, geisha." There was a warn-ing note in Helen's voice as she mashed out her ciga-rette and stood up. She flashed me a stony stare, then left.

I followed her with my eyes. There was never a girl whom I feared, but I did not care for trouble. I wanted to be happy here. When I turned back to the table Colette was smiling at me.

"I hope I didn't make her angry," I said.

"Helen is just naturally a jealous girl. She thinks all men should go for big blondes."

"But I can't help that, nor can you," I said.

"The trouble is," Colette explained, "most of the men from the mainland who come here want something dif-ferent. They'll select a girl like Lemomie, or Vanessa or me. And I imagine you'll get a play from them too. Helen is popular enough with local customers. But it's the vacationers who leave the big tips."

"Then the blame is on them."

"Look, just take my advice and leave Helen alone. She'll cause you a lot of trouble if you don't," said Co-lette quietly.

"I'll do that," I promised.

On the way to my room Mrs. Reisner called me into the office. She did not ask me to sit down.

"Since your album won't be ready until tomorrow you won't be made available to all visitors tonight. But be prepared to entertain nevertheless. Maybe two or three. You'll have no all night visitors. There's a buzzer by the door. Just press it when ordering drinks for your guests. Lillian or Grace, the other Filipino girl, will be at your service."

"Thank you, Mrs. Reisner. And I hope I shall prove worthy of your employment."

"Use your charms in the right way and you will."

18

At nine o'clock Lillian knocked at my door and informed me that a visitor would be brought to me shortly. Since I had not been instructed as to what garment to wear, I put on the kimono. It made me feel confident and at ease. I assessed myself critically in the mirror. My excitement was not for what was about to happen. It was for my success as a geisha in another land. If I could please my first gentleman-san, it would be a good omen for continued success at Mrs. Reisner's.

CHAPTER THREE

The men I entertained at Mrs. Reisner's during the next few weeks were Americans, for the most part. They were big, gay men like the ones I had entertained in the geisha house in Tokyo. But here they dispensed with all ceremony. Once in a while one would wish a drink, and then we would sit at the cocktail table and talk, but not for long. They were impetuous and strong. Their desires were quickly dissipated.

One evening Mr. Yukio, a Japanese, visited me and said he had learned that I had been a geisha in the homeland. We spoke to each other in Japanese and I assured him that what he had learned was true. We visited a long time that evening about places in Japan that were familiar to us both. He was delighted when I promised to perform the tea ceremonial, Cha-no-yu, for him one evening when he returned.

Mr. Yukio became a regular visitor. We enjoyed Cha-no-yu together, kneeling on the tatami with the furo, the water jar and the chakin before us. He was highly complimentary of my etiquette in serving him the tea bowl. It is a ritual with which every well-trained geisha is familiar.

I was pleased to be able to practice more than just one portion of the geisha art and Mr. Yukio's visits were always welcome. But I was startled to learn one day that his seeing me so regularly had upset the other

20

girls. Betty Richards came to my room and asked me for the secret.

"What secret?" I asked, looking at her in bewilderment.

"You've been here less than a month, but already you've built up a steady trade. I've been here nearly a year and the only steady I've got is an old guy who says I look like the girl he wanted to marry but lost."

I looked at Betty. She was a pretty girl and young, but hard lines were already showing on her face. She was always at pains to conceal her drinking from Mrs. Reisner. The chances were that such a one would burn herself out quickly. I smiled and shrugged.

"I have no secret, Betty."

"You've got something," said the girl, lighting a cigarette and propping her feet up on the cocktail table. "You got that Jap importer away from Helen. He'd been visiting her steadily for months and never touched another girl until you came along."

"Mr. Yukio? I didn't know he liked Helen."

"Sure he did. And he's a free spender. Helen is sore as a goat about losing him."

"I hope she doesn't blame me. I had nothing to do with it. He visits me mainly for Cha-no-yu."

"For what?" Betty's feet hit the floor with a bang. She sat up and looked at me closely.

"The tea ceremony."

"Is that what you do with all those kitchen utensils you borrow from Mrs. Reisner?"

"Yes. She knows what Mr. Yukio and I do."

"Is that all you do?" Betty's eyes twinkled.

"No. Certainly not."

I knew what she was thinking. She would have been surprised to know that Mr. Yukio brought Japanese poetry and read it to me, and that we spent much time discussing landscape painting, and music and flower

21

arranging. What Betty and the other girls did not know is that the possession of one's body is but a single function of the geisha.

When Betty left I walked to the window and looked out, but I did not see the lovely valley nor the Aloha Tower rising above the Honolulu Harbor beyond. It suddenly occurred to me that I had not been completely accepted by the girls. They had been friendly enough, but now I remembered the speculative glances that had come my way on more than one occasion. I was not one of them. It was something that I must correct.

But I did not realize the obstacles in the way toward a closer comaraderie with them. They continued to view me with some feeling of suspicion and mistrust. I knew I must learn their ways gradually and meanwhile it was easier to make no intrusions.

During my free time, and always with Mrs. Reisner's permission, I roamed Oahu, seeing the sights of the island and of Honolulu sprawled along the leeward shore and pushing its streets and homes up into the valleys of the Koolau mountains. I reasoned that it was a good way to get to know western people better and to make myself one of them.

These excursions, even though I lacked companionship, proved to be unusually pleasant. I had never known such freedom. It never ceased to amaze me that I could stand on the Aiea Heights and gaze down at the great naval base at Pearl Harbor without being told by a guard to move on. I watched planes from all over the world land and take off from Honolulu airport and not once did I see passengers stopped and questioned.

I stood with other sightseers in the wind of the Pali and gazed out over green valley and blue ocean. I explored the shops of Honolulu, watched the ships dock with their mainland passengers, among the most festive expressions of goodwill I had ever seen. I bought a bathing suit and swam at Waikiki. And I learned what the wolf whistle meant.

I was careful not to encourage the men who whistled at me. Mrs. Reisner had warned me about that. I was to make no alliances outside of the house on pain of instant dismissal. However, one afternoon at Waikiki, I was involved before I realized what had happened.

I was sitting on the seawall, gazing out beyond the reef toward the swelling waters of the Pacific. I had spent half an hour in the surf and was sunning myself and all at once I heard movement beside me. I looked around to see a young American man in a bright aloha shirt sitting beside me.

"Hello," he said with such a friendly, warm-hearted smile that he was impossible to ignore. He had light hair, clear blue eyes and a slender build.

I was so surprised that I could think of nothing to say. I looked at him, wondering if I might have had him for a customer without remembering him.

"My name is Gil Dawson. I just happened to be strolling by and you looked a bit lonesome. Are you, I hope?"

"Well, I'm alone, if that's what you mean."

"I'm glad you're by yourself. So am I. At least, I was. If you mentioned your name I failed to catch it."

He was so much at ease that it seemed only natural that I should tell him my name.

"It's Kimiko," I said.

"What a pretty name," he replied, after thinking it over a minute. He regarded me curiously. "Where are you from?"

"Japan. Where are you from?" I thought it best to get him to talk about himself if we were to have a brief visit.

"Centralia, Illinois."

"Where is that?"

23

"The central part of the state," he answered.

"Where is Illinois?"

He looked at me quickly. "Are you kidding? You don't know where Illinois is?"

"I never heard of it."

He stared at me. I looked back at him, frankly interested in learning about his native land. My aunt had taught me good speech and some writing, but I was woefully lacking in geography.

"Well, I'll be damned! Illinois is right in the middle of the United States and Centralia is right in the middle of that. Now do you know where it is?" he laughed.

"In the middle." The smile I gave him was over my own ignorance.

"You should go to America sometime."

"I'd love to," I said truthfully. "I have heard so much about that big country."

"If you're interested I'll tell you a lot more." Before I could stop him he launched into a colorful description of his country, from the towering skyscrapers of New York to the vast plains and mountains of the far west.

. Not many men could have held my interest for an hour, as he did. Gil Dawson was an artful conversationalist and his enthusiasm was contagious. The time passed so quickly that I failed to realize that I must be getting back to the house for dinner.

"Why don't you get dressed and let's go have a cocktail together? I'll tell you more," he said finally.

"What time is it?" I gasped, remembering that I had planned to start home much earlier.

"Only a little after five."

I jumped down from the seawall. "I must hurry."

"But why?"

"I—I have an appointment."

"Could I see you later this evening?"

24

"No, I'm afraid not."

"Then let me drive you to your appointment," he suggested hopefully.

"No. This will have to end it for today," I said without thinking.

He snatched at the opening. "Good, then let's meet here again tomorrow."

"I'm sorry." I was truly regretful that I would not see him again. He had been so kind and considerate and interesting. He was like Mr. Yukio, but much younger and much better looking.

"Day after tomorrow, then," he persisted.

"I can't say."

"You can say whether you'll ever come back to this spot some afternoon. And if you do, I'll be waiting, no matter how long it may be."

"Maybe I will." I was not being honest with myself or him. I knew I should never come back here to see him. It was a worse mistake to offer him encouragement. I wondered what had gotten into me.

Quickly I walked away, up the beach, toward the bathhouse where I had changed into my swim suit. I stole a glance at him over my shoulder. He was still standing on the seawall and he waved the instant I turned. Impulsively I waved back. Even at that distance his smile was disarming.

I hurried into my street dress and rather than be late for dinner I took a taxi from Waikiki. In my mind's eye I could still see him waving. I cherished that picture, for I had found him so likeable. But I told myself repeatedly that I must never go back. I had come to know that in Hawaii girls of my profession did not take up with young men like that.

Later that evening, after entertaining my first visitor from eight-thirty to nine-thirty, Mrs. Reisner sent word that I would have an all night guest from ten o'clock on. I bathed and refreshed myself, then changed into an evening dress and was ready when he arrived. He was an American in his middle thirties with dark hair and nice features.

"You're every bit as enticing as your pictures the woman downstairs showed me," he said, looking me over.

"Thank you." I bowed and smiled. "Americans say such nice things."

I wanted to talk about America and was delighted when he asked if drinks could be sent up for us. Lillian brought ice and a bottle of Scotch whiskey. I made the drinks for my guest then sat down across from him at the cocktail table.

"Are you by any chance from Illinois?" I asked.

"No. Ohio. But I've been in Illinois a lot. Why, do you know that state?"

I shook my head. "Are the men in Illinois like those in Ohio?"

"Probably so," he laughed.

I had heard that in America prostitution was looked upon with much disfavor, and that there was no place in the scheme of things for geishas or concubines. I had always been puzzled by that, since American men showed no lack of interest in women.

"Do men patronize girls there?" I asked.

"Yes."

"What do they think of them?"

"What do men think about the girls they patronize?" He smiled peculiarly. I nodded and he went on, somewhat hesitantly. "Well, I can't exactly say. Americans don't approve of girls who—" Suddenly he stopped and frowned. "Hell, I'm only speaking for myself and as far as you're concerned I like your looks."

I sat back in my chair and crossed my legs. I was pensive over what he had told me as I sipped my drink.

26

What would Gil Dawson have said to that, I wondered.

"Are Illinois men like that too?" I asked.

"They're like anybody else."

Suddenly he grinned at me and reached out. His hand traveled up my leg and patted the bare flesh of my thigh above the top of my stocking.

"I can look at a girl in an evening dress any time. Why don't you take it off?"

Suddenly I felt apologetic. I was not being a good hostess, inflicting my own thoughts upon him. I smiled and stood up. I removed the dress and hung it away in the closet. His eyes lit up as I stood before him in the black bra, panties and stockings. This was what he had come here for, not to get confused about what Illinois men thought of girls like me. I took his empty glass and made him another drink.

There were many other questions I would have liked to ask but now I must please. He had confirmed what I had learned on other occasions. It was strange that American men would come to girls at Mrs. Reisner's, and condemn them after taking their enjoyment. Strange, but not for me to question.

Later, when the lights were out and I held him in my arms, his passion showed no signs of disapproval whatsoever. He had drunk too much for his own good but he was vigorous, like most Americans. When the night brought him contentment and he drifted off into slumber, I stroked his shoulders and chest as he lay at my side. But I was not thinking of him as I gazed up into the darkness. I was thinking of the young man from Illinois.

CHAPTER FOUR

Loneliness was a new experience for me. I had always enjoyed the tranquility of solitude. During the moments when I was alone in my room I was never bored. I loved the ancient art of *Ikebana* and delighted in the subtle moods of gentility and serenity that could be achieved with flower arrangement. A few branches, a bit of greenery and a flower or two in a flat vase could occupy me happily for hours.

But the loneliness that gradually seeped into my mind and spirit was not relieved. It was there when I sunned myself on the lanai in the company of Vanessa, Betty, Helen and the others. It was there, even more so, during my intimate companionship with guests.

Once I awakened in the dark hours of early morning with an unaccountably heavy heart. An all night guest lay at my side. In his slumber he had enmeshed one of my legs in his and I could not move without disturbing him. I rolled my head on the pillow and looked up through the window at the high, wan stars. Suddenly I knew the truth of my loneliness.

I had been tempted, during my time off in the afternoons, to return to Waikiki, but my better judgment had prevailed. Becoming friendly with the young man from Illinois could lead nowhere. His interest in me would collapse the instant he learned how I was employed. Either that, or he might come to me as a guest. I preferred to keep our hour together out of my routine world. It gave me something to remember, something a little nice to think about when I was dealing with lust.

What insane motive it was that drew me back to our trysting place on the seawall at Waikiki ten days later, I could never explain. I had been swimming for an hour and still had plenty of time left that afternoon before I had to return to the house. I wandered over and sat down. I did not look around for a glimpse of the young man, knowing that if he had come back the day following our meeting, he had given me up after all this time. Oddly enough I didn't even think of him as I sat there watching a surfboard rider skillfully maneuver his craft before an onrushing wave.

"Kimiko!"

The sound of my name broke into my subconscious mind with such force that I jumped. I looked around quickly. Gil Dawson ran up to me. His face was alive with eagerness.

"You did come back, after all. Just as you said!" he exclaimed.

"Hello." I was at once both sorry and glad that he had found me.

"Golly, I'd given up days ago. Do you know I was passing here just by chance this very moment?" he said.

"I thought you would be back in Illinois by now." It was all I could think to say.

"Not me!" His eyes swarmed over my face and his grin stretched all the way across his cheeks. "I'm here to stay. And right now I'm here with you and you're not going to get away this time without letting me know more about you."

I got down from the seawall. It had been a bad mistake to come here again. It was time to walk out of his life forever.

"I'm sorry, Gil. I shouldn't have met you."

29

"Why not?" he asked, jumping down beside me.

"Many reasons. I have to go now." I looked down at the sand, wishing that what I had said was not so.

"No you don't!" He grabbed my wrist. "You wouldn't have come back if you weren't willing to see me. Where do you live? Where can I reach you? You've got to learn a lot more about geography. Remember?" He grinned.

"Please let me go. This is all wrong." My heart was beginning to pound.

"What's your last name?"

"Omura." I could be honest with him to that extent.

"Are you going to tell me where you live or will I have to come with you and find out for myself?"

"You can't do that," I cried in alarm.

"Would your parents be that disapproving of me?"

"No. It isn't that, Gil."

"I'm not going to lose track of you this time. That's for sure." He was pleasant about it, but firm.

My mind raced. I could not have him going with me to Mrs. Reisner's. It might jeopardize my employment if she learned that I had met him through a flirtation on the beach. Only one solution came to me.

"If you let me go I'll promise to meet you here again. If that's what you want," I said.

"I want a lot more but if that's the best I can do—well, it's a bargain." He let go of my wrist. "Tomorrow at two o'clock. Can you make it?"

If I got up at noon I could make it. It was not the right thing to do, but I had brought this on myself. I looked at him. Surely seeing him one more time would not result in tragedy.

"Yes. I'll come."

"Promise?" He eyed me questioningly.

"I don't go back on my word."

"Swell!" he exclaimed, delighted. "We'll have a swim.

30

Then later on, some cocktails. How about dinner at the Royal?"

"No. I'm sorry. We'll just have to be together right here. Nothing more."

"But we could go over to my place. There would be no harm in that. I live only two blocks away."

"For now let's just agree to meet here at two," I said, avoiding his eyes.

This time, as I walked away, I did not glance back. It was enough to have tomorrow to think about. I did not let my thoughts go beyond that, for there must be no more visits with Gil. It had to be that way, for his sake and mine. But for the next twenty-four hours I could live in happiness and anticipation. I must seek other ways to overcome loneliness—after tomorrow.

CHAPTER FIVE

The Waikiki bus swung over to the curb and stopped. I was among several passengers who got off. Two sailors whistled at me covetously as I moved along the sidewalk with quick strides. I ignored them. It was ten minutes after two and I hurried to keep my appointment with Gil.

I wished I could have postponed our afternoon date. I had not gone to sleep until four-thirty that morning. I hoped the weariness did not show in my eyes, nor my cheeks. I was dressed in a yellow print dress, open at the collar and belted around the waist. I carried my swim suit in a small bag.

"Sorry I'm late, but I missed the first bus," I said, coming up to him at our seawall meeting place.

"I'd have waited hours," Gil grinned. This was the first time he had ever seen me in anything but a bathing suit. I could tell by his eyes that he was pleased with my appearance. "Do you especially want to be on the beach this afternoon? My car is right across the street. I thought we might take a ride up on Tantalus and then come back to my place."

His suggestion appealed to me. I had heard of the Tantalus drive but had never been there. It would be something different. I could see no harm in it, since we were to be together anyway.

"I'd love that," I told him.

32

He helped me into his convertible, then hurried around and slid under the wheel. I relaxed against the cushions and the wind brushed back my hair as we drove off. I was happy that I had kept the date. Taking a drive with Gil was exciting. The only car I had been in on Oahu was Mrs. Reisner's.

"Have you ever been to Tantalus?" he asked.

"No."

"Then you've got a treat in store. There's nothing like learning local geography before we skip all the way back to the mainland."

"That suits me fine," I smiled.

We drove through a section of Honolulu that I did not know existed. The road began a precipitous ascent. We passed many beautiful houses, hanging high on the mountain side. I was reminded of the country around Tokyo. The car climbed for fifteen minutes and Gil stopped at a wide observation point.

I looked out over the incredibly beautiful Manoa Valley. He pointed out the Ala Wai and Waikiki where we had been only a few minutes ago. Farther beyond was Diamond Head, lying massive and Sphinx-like in the afternoon sun. I was entranced with the view.

"Now I know what people mean when they speak of glorious Tantalus," I said.

"Are you sure?" Gil smiled slowly. His arm was resting behind me, along the top of the seat. "This is a popular place to come after dark. So popular that it's difficult to find a place to park."

His fingers brushed the back of my neck and sent a tiny tingle down my spine as he turned and started the engine. The road continued upward until it seemed lost in the mountains. We drove through dense forests and presently started down the opposite side. Gil stopped the car again as the road crawled dangerously along the top of a sharp ridge which dropped down abruptly on both sides to the valley hundreds of feet below.

"Over there is Pearl Harbor," he said, pointing.

I shaded my eyes from the sun in order to see it. I could barely make out the ships which seemed like tiny toys at such a distance. I looked down into the valley below. The winding road had mixed up my directions.

"What valley is this?" I asked.

"Nuuanu," Gil replied.

I gave a start. All at once I looked intently at the houses that were half buried from view in their surrounding greenery. After a moment I was able to identify the large green roof of Mrs. Reisner's establishment. I stared, fascinated for a few seconds, then turned to Gil.

"Shall we go now?" I said quickly.

"What's the matter, are you getting dizzy?" he laughed.

"Yes." Only it was not the way he thought.

We descended into Honolulu. Instead of returning to Waikiki by the same route, Gil drove out to Beretania, past the Academy of Arts and the University and went over to the Beach on Kapahulu Avenue. It was three-thirty when he stopped in front of a one-story, U-shaped apartment building, two blocks from the beach.

"This is where I live, Kimiko. I made some punch before I left. It should be good and cold by now. Would you like some?"

"If you wish."

I had enjoyed the ride so much that all my caution was gone. He got out and opened the door for me. We walked through a small courtyard. He opened the door and welcomed me into his home.

I stood in the room looking around. I understood immediately that Gil Dawson was not a man of wealth, but it made no difference to me whatever. The place was homey, cheerful and comfortable. I stared curiously at the paintings on the wall. They were watercolors of schooners and palms and the ocean. I looked at his books and magazines on a small, low table.

"Have you read any of those?" he asked conversationally as he went toward the kitchen.

"Oh no."

"Sit down. Make yourself comfortable. I'll be right back with the punch."

I seated myself in an easy chair. While he was gone a strange feeling came over me. It was as if this room was somehow familiar. Yet, it was unlike any in which I had lived my life. Could I have known it in a dream? For a breathless instant I felt that I belonged here. Then the magic was gone. I was faintly amused at my own fantasy. I knew that I could never belong to a room like this.

"Here you are," said Gil, handing me a glass.

I took a sip. It was good; but it was flavored with gin. I had to be careful. It would be fatal to return to Mrs. Reisner's with the odor of liquor on my breath. I smiled and put the glass down on the table.

"Don't you like it?" Gil asked quickly.

"It's delicious."

He sat down. I complimented him on his apartment. He laughed and explained that it was purely temporary. As soon as he found himself a business he was going to move into roomier quarters. He even speculated about buying a little house. He told me that he had become interested in the Hawaiian Islands during a tour of duty in the Navy. After his enlistment was over he had come back here to make his home, after an uncle had died and left him a small inheritance. We had not been talking long when someone called through the door.

"Hi, Gil. Are you home?"

"Sure am. Come on over," he called back.

In a moment a most attractive Chinese girl came in. I was introduced to Audrey Ching. She studied me curiously for a moment. All at once she turned to Gil.

"I didn't know you had company. Perhaps I'd better come back later." Her eyes sparkled with mirth.

"Have a drink before you go," he grinned.

"Gladly."

I marveled at the Chinese girl's perfect English. She was graceful and relaxed and altogether a pleasant person.

"Do you live near here, Kimiko?" Audrey asked.

"Well," I hesitated a second, "I live in Honolulu."

"Do you like it?"

"I think it is quite a lovely city," I replied, my glance traveling to Gil. This girl behaved as if she knew something about me. Gil must have told her. My eyes returned to Audrey. "Has this been your home long?"

"All my life. I was born and raised right here on Oahu."

We talked on. I had little to contribute to the conversation. I was aware of the appraising looks the girl gave me from time to time but did not resent them. There was something rather warm and understanding about Audrey Ching.

"I've got to trot along," she said, finishing her drink. She stood up. "Come back and see us again soon, Kimiko. If Gil won't let you in, come to my place. I'm right next door."

Her congenial laughter went with her out of the apartment. When she was gone Gil returned to his chair. He looked across at me and smiled.

"Audrey is a swell girl. Her only trouble is, she's in the wrong business."

"What is that?" I asked out of politeness.

"To put it bluntly, she's a call girl, if you know what I mean. She's available for luaus, does hula dances and can be had if the price is right. It's sort of odd having a girl like that as a neighbor, but she's fun nevertheless. I kid her a lot, but she loves it."

I had stiffened at the mention of "call girl." I knew what it meant only too well. I studied Gil closely. I did not know whether he was being subtle or just plain naive.

"I hope you're not offended," he said.

"Goodness no!" I said quickly.

Gil was entirely unaware of the thoughts that raced through my mind. He talked on.

"It's a damn shame that a girl like Audrey can't do better than that. It's not an easy life. Sometimes she's dragging home just as I'm getting up in the morning."

"That's normal to one of her calling," I said guardedly.

- "I know, but there ought to be an easier way for a girl to make a living."

I didn't know what to think about Gil Dawson. At first I feared that his reference to Audrey Ching was leading to a revelation that he had learned the truth about me. But now I sensed from his attitude that he was merely expressing his opinion of Audrey. And the astounding thing about it was that he was sincere in his concern. Suddenly he looked at me and smiled.

"But at that it's better than working in some of the dives around Honolulu. Audrey is independent. I'd say she's better than the other kind, even though she's marked by the same brand."

"You disapprove of what she does to make a living?" I asked.

"My attitude is that it's none of my business."

I stared into space. Gil was like other American men I had heard about. I liked him none the less for it. It was a matter of custom, and the acceptance of century-old habits. But it made me feel a sudden and heavy

37

melancholy. If he felt that way about Audrey Ching, how would he feel about me? The answer was apparent. It might hurt him to learn the truth about me. It strengthened my resolve never to see him again after this afternoon.

"That's a good way to be, Gil," I said.

He arose and took my glass. I was surprised to discover that I had emptied it while we talked. He started toward the kitchen. I jumped up and ran after him.

"No more for me, please. I've got to be going."

He looked around. His eyes filled with protest. "But it's still only mid-afternoon. Surely you don't have to go this early!"

"Yes. I must."

"But—" He eyed me sternly, smiling a little. "No! I won't have it. You promised me a date this afternoon. It was a bargain we made. Remember?"

He ignored my objections and refilled the glasses. I was careful to take only a tiny sip then set it down. Gil began to question me. He was not prying. He was genuinely interested. At first I had difficulty avoiding answers I did not wish to give, but long practice in the art of the geisha had taught me how to get men to talk about themselves. Soon Gil was rambling on about his college days, his hopes of settling in Hawaii and a myriad of other subjects which I encouraged by giving him my complete attention.

He had drunk more than I and paid no attention to the time. I was careful to watch that.

"Our afternoon must end now, Gil. I must go," I said finally.

We were sitting on the studio couch and he had been showing me snapshots taken at his home back in Illinois. I handed him the pictures.

"Have dinner with me tonight," he pleaded.

"I'm sorry but I can't do that."

38

His arm slipped around me. "When will you, Kimiko? Can't you see I've simply got to know you better?"

"It's best not to think that way," I told him, trying to keep the sadness out of my voice.

"But why? Why?" he asked.

I looked into his eyes. For a second I was on the verge of confessing to him. But then, I realized, it would be best to leave him and let him remember me as he might prefer.

His arm tightened about my waist; I realized that he was drawing me to him. I was about to insist that he release me when his lips exploded on mine. I was powerless to resist his eagerness as he held me tightly in his arms.

"Please let me go now," I said, pushing against him.

He did not yield his grasp on me. I saw the yearning in his eyes and felt the pounding of his heart. I grew alarmed. The last thing I had intended doing was arouse him. He forced me back and pushed the fullness of my skirt out of his way.

I had submitted to such advances on countless occasions but this time I had to resist. It was not fair to him.

"No, Gil. Don't," I begged.

"But, Kimi—"

He broke off. His questioning eyes looked down at me. They were filled with desire. I felt his hands on me and suddenly it was beyond my power to deny him. I wanted to give him happiness. It made no difference if his regard turned to bitterness later on. I entwined my arms around his neck and knew the thrill of holding him close. I guided my lips to his and gave him a long kiss.

It wasn't until later that I became aware of the pounding of my own heart. I suddenly realized that I wanted him greedily, hungrily now. As my own emo-

39

tion surged beyond control I gave myself to him without restraint. At last I had found someone whose desire awakened my response.

"I've got to go now, Gil. I simply must. Please let me," I said, a long time later.

"Where are you going?" he kissed my cheek and smiled.

"Home."

"I'll take you."

"No. I must say good-bye right here."

"Hell, no!" He took immediate exception to that.

"But you can't go with me."

"Why?"

"Because I don't want you to," I said, looking up at him gravely.

"Why are you so mysterious with me?" he asked.

"I'm not. Move. I've already stayed too long."

"Tell me why I can't drive you home," he said, refusing to let go of me.

"Please, Gil." I beseeched him with my eyes.

His resolve melted. But he held me a moment more. "If you won't let me take you home, you'll have to promise to come back."

"I—I can't."

"Very well, then. You'll stay right here until you change your mind."

I was distressed. There was no choice but to promise to return. With that he let me up. Quickly I straightened my hair and my dress, smoothing it down over my knees.

"How about tomorrow afternoon? Same time. Same place," he asked.

"Not tomorrow."

"When?"

"Three days from now," I said. It made no difference.

40

"I have your word," he reminded me.

"Yes, Gil." A promise forced was no promise.

He kissed me again before I left. I felt a pang in my heart as I turned away and hurried toward Kalakaua Avenue. I was not concerned that I was going to deceive him. It was for his own good. But that final kiss had weakened my resolve. I had to get hold of myself. I could not permit myself to fall in love with that boy. Such an unholy alliance could lead only to heartbreak for us both.

Yet, the touch of his lips lingered on mine, as if emblazoned forever on my soul.

CHAPTER SIX

Mrs. Reisner and the other girls were at dinner when I hurried in. I glanced at her as I sat down and got a long, speculative look in return. She waited until my food was served before she said anything.

"Where were you that you couldn't get back in time to sit down with the rest of us?" she asked.

"I was swimming at Waikiki and lost track of the time, Mrs. Reisner." It was the first time I had ever lied to her and it made me hot with shame.

"Try not to let it happen again," Mrs. Reisner advised coolly.

Nothing more was said. One or two of the girls glanced in my direction and Helen regarded me calculatingly. But the others ignored it. The talk, as usual, was about clothes and current topics of the day.

I was the last to finish my dessert and leave the table. I picked up my bag, for I hadn't taken the time to run up to my room with it before dinner. Upstairs I entered my room and had barely closed the door behind me when Helen walked in. I tossed the bag to the dresser.

"You want something, Helen?" I inquired.

She smiled coldly. "Nothing in particular. Just paying a friendly visit."

I studied her quietly. There was nothing friendly in the girl's hostile eyes. She had some perverse reason for being here but I couldn't tell what it was. I waited a moment to see what she would say. When she remained silent I shrugged. I lifted my skirt and pulled it off over my head. When I glanced at Helen again, she was over at the dresser removing my swim suit from the bag.

"What's the meaning of that?" I demanded.

Helen glanced at me scornfully. She held the swim suit up in her hand. "It doesn't feel the least bit damp. It must have dried awfully quickly after your swim."

I grabbed the suit away from her. "Let my things alone!"

"Who are you trying to kid? You haven't been near the water this afternoon," said Helen with contempt.

"It's none of your business," I retorted.

"I've noticed you spend most afternoons away from here. What're you doing, working for the Sandman down on River Street during your time off?"

The Sandman's was one of the more notorious dives in town, not really on River Street, but close enough to be identified with it. I had heard the girls talk a lot about the place. It was not the kind of establishment I would care to work in. For a girl to leave Mrs. Reisner's and become an inmate of the Sandman's was a step down in the peculiar stratification of a profession thought by some to have no lower levels.

"I don't even answer such stupid accusations," I replied with as much dignity as I could.

"You might to Evaline Reisner one of these days," Helen predicted.

"And if I do it will still be none of your business." The other girls might recognize Helen as a leader, but not me.

Helen's eyes blazed. "There's plenty that's my business and don't you ever forget it! I'm sick and tired of

43

the play you've made for all the best customers in this joint. And I'm not the only one!"

"Will you please leave now?"

The girl shook with fury. For an instant I feared that she might start a fight. Helen was large and strong. She would be difficult to ward off, even with the uses of jujitsu in which I'd had some training. All at once she gained control of herself. She tossed me a hateful glance then left the room.

I pondered the incident. Clearly, Helen Gray was after me. Her visit had been premeditated, to check on my story. And the dry swim suit had given her the information she needed. Without supporting evidence, Helen could do nothing. It would not end there, however. It was only the beginning. I had to watch my step with Helen. At the first sign of my weakness, the girl would spring with the fury of a tiger.

My work day began at eight o'clock that evening. I put Helen out of my mind and gave my attention to the gentlemen-san who sought relaxation. I did not have the same success in dismissing Gil from my mind.

As the evening wore on and other companions visited me, my thoughts wandered back to the small apartment at Waikiki. What had happened there was a thing apart from what was happening tonight. I had been receptive to Gil's rapture and had shared the ecstacy of his embrace. I had been a different girl. With Gil I had known the real meaning of mutual desire. Here, I responded only with carefully controlled simulation.

Try as I did, for the next three days, I was unable to forget Gil. I conjured up every reason under the sun to bolster my resolve not to return to Waikiki. The affair must not continue. Any fool could see that. And yet, I wanted to return as I had promised to do.

I was at the seawall at two o'clock three days later. That launched a series of afternoon dates which

44

I was helpless to break off. I lived in a different world when I was with Gil. And I loved that world with its broad view of happiness and enchantment, even though I knew it never could last.

Gil tried to find out why I limited our dates to the afternoons. I had to threaten not to see him again if he did not let well enough alone.

I became better acquainted with Audrey Ching, and exceedingly fond of her. That lively, good-hearted girl was in and out a great deal when I was with Gil at his apartment. Once, when Gil had gone to a store, leaving Audrey and me alone for a few minutes, she told me that he was in love with me. I told her that was wrong and she agreed, but she did not ask why. She also told me a thing about Gil that I had never known. He had been in love once back in the United States, but had lost out. That was one of the reasons he wanted to make Hawaii his home. I felt more sympathy and understanding toward him than ever.

I was thinking of him as I was sunning myself on a beach towel spread on the grass behind the house one afternoon. Betty and Vanessa were lying nearby. Mrs. Reisner permitted us to sunbathe there, where the protective shrubbery concealed us from view. Helen sat in a deck chair, her head wrapped in a towel.

"How come you didn't go swimming this afternoon?" Helen asked.

I did not reply. Helen spoke again for Betty's and Vanessa's benefit.

"Well, I guess that's understandable. I'd forgotten today was Monday. There's not much doing at the Sandman's or any other place." She laughed at her oblique reference to my extra-curricular duties. But instead of ending it there she kept talking. She even asked Betty and Vanessa what they had done about the men she claimed I had stolen from them. Neither girl replied.

45

"Please be quiet, Helen," I said, when I had listened to her taunts as long as I could.

"Listen to who's giving orders!" Helen snapped.

At that moment Lemomie came out of the house and joined us in the sun.

"Be careful," Helen warned her. "Kimiko might make you leave if she doesn't like the way your hair is parted."

"What?" asked Lemomie, ignorant of what had been going on.

"That one," Helen gestured contemptuously at me. "She's made herself the prima donna of this joint."

"You'd better not talk so loud. Mrs. Reisner might not like it," Lemomie pointed out.

"She went to the bank this afternoon. Anyway, I'm no more afraid of her than I am of the hot shot from Tokyo. You never did say why you left there, Kimiko. What did they do, kick you out?"

I was lying face down, trying to rest. Exasperated, I sat up on the beach towel and eyed her.

"I didn't come out here to bother you or be bothered. What you say means nothing to me. It's only your manner that is irritating. If you wish to say something more, do it and get it over with. Then let me alone."

"I've got plenty more to say! I'm speaking for the others, too. We're tired of you. Before you showed up we didn't have any trouble. Why don't you get wise? Get out before we force Reisner to do something about you," Helen shot back.

I stared at her. I had never suspected that the other girls disliked me. I looked around. Lemomie avoided my eyes. The other two had sat up.

"Is she right? Is she speaking for all of you?" I asked.

No one replied. I didn't know whether they had a grievance against me, or whether they simply wished to stay out of the argument. Finally Betty spoke.

46

"Don't get involved, either one of you."

Helen glared at the small blonde. "You told me she had taken some of your trade."

"I've got enough," Betty replied.

Seeing that Helen's talk was that of a self-appointed leader, I turned to her. "You'll save everyone trouble if you shut up now."

With that I adjusted the beach towel and lay back. I folded my arms under my head and closed my eyes. In a moment I heard movement beside me. I looked up to see Helen standing over me. I had underestimated the girl's pent-up wrath. I saw savage fury in her eyes.

Suddenly the girl leaped upon me. With a sudden surge of fear I tried to roll aside. I was a second too late. Her weight knocked the breath out of me. Pain stabbed through me as Helen grabbed my hair and jerked my head back violently. I cried out.

"I'll make you eat those words!" Helen cried, clawing at me.

All thoughts were driven from my head except that of survival. My strength arose on a welling tide of terror. I fought back instinctively as we rolled on the grass. The other girls had leaped up. They stood around us, looking on with horror but fearing to intervene lest they too become implicated.

Helen's superior size gave her an advantage over me. She struck me viciously. I felt hot, seering agony with each blow. All at once I felt my breathing shut off. Helen had fastened her legs around my body. They were constricting against me with deadly pressure. She was trying to kill me, I thought in a frenzy. I grabbed out blindly. My hands found her foot. I applied a jujitsu leverage that came back to me instinctively. For a moment we both writhed in a torture neither of us could break.

At that instant Joe, the gardener, rounded the corner

47

of the house at top speed. He had been watering some orchids when he heard our screams. He pushed Betty and Vanessa aside and bent over us. It took him a moment to pry us apart. The instant I was free I leaped up, breathing heavily and in great gasps but still ready to defend myself. Helen sobbed as she lay on the ground holding her ankle. If it wasn't broken it was badly sprained, for I had twisted it viciously.

"Who started this?" Joe demanded.

Not a sound came from the girls. He glared around at them. During this short interval I regained my senses.

"Helen started it," I said.

Still the girls would not speak. But one or two heads gave short nods, confirming what I had said. Helen was still on the ground, weeping hysterically. She did not know what was going on. Both of us were the worse for the melee. I had suffered a three-inch-long gash across my shoulder. Helen's ankle was beginning to swell. Suddenly the commanding voice of Mrs. Reisner rang out. We all turned and looked as she ran across the lanai.

When she saw the condition of Helen and me she roared with anger. "Somebody is going to regret this. You can all be damned sure of that! Now get to your rooms, every one of you, and stay there until I send for you!"

CHAPTER SEVEN

Mrs. Reisner began her investigation at once. She sat in her office and questioned each witness to the fight one at a time. Then she called Helen, and finally me.

As I waited in my room I tried to compose myself. I ached where Helen had struck me and the gash in my shoulder stung, but it was not the physical pain that concerned me most. It was the agitation in my mind. It would only cause more trouble for me if I let emotion dictate what I would say to Mrs. Reisner. I wanted to be truthful with her above all else.

I speculated gloomily on what would happen if I was dismissed. There was no one in all Hawaii that I could turn to for help. The only value I had was the pleasure I afforded men. Perhaps my services could be utilized in the establishments along River Street. My pride would suffer but at this point I had very little left.

"Mrs. Reisner will see you now," said Lillian appearing at my door half an hour later.

I went downstairs to the office. Mrs. Reisner sat behind her desk, her eyes hard and unyielding. She would dispense justice as she saw it and nothing on earth would change her mind.

"I'm sorry, Mrs. Reisner. I never intended to cause trouble when Captain Hagan-san brought me here," I said immediately.

49

She waved me to a chair. I sat down. I felt abashed under her stern and unsympathetic gaze.

"What happened?" was all she said.

"I'm afraid Helen and I can't get along. I'll leave if you think best. She doesn't like me. It's partly my fault but I can't help it."

"Can't help what?"

"She accuses me of attracting some of her more steady patrons away from her. I was not aware of doing so."

"How did the fight start?" Mrs. Reisner asked, after a short silence during which she studied me closely.

I told her exactly what had happened as I remembered it. What I related took less than a couple of minutes. When I finished Mrs. Reisner asked me another question.

"You are accusing Helen of instigating the fight, are you not?"

"I only told what happened. She hit me first. That is true. But I made the mistake of quarreling with her before we clashed. I should have gone to my room when I saw the mood she was in. That way it would have all been avoided."

"Helen made some accusations about you. She said you do not spend your afternoons swimming at Waikiki, as you have said. She said you made extra money entertaining customers somewhere during your time off. Is that true?"

"No. It is false."

"Go to your room. I don't want you talking to anyone until you're told you may," said Mrs. Reisner abruptly.

Tears came unbidden when I was once again in my room. I had not lied to Mrs. Reisner, yet her question had given me an out. For that I was ashamed. Perhaps I should have confessed everything. Maybe I should have told her about Gil. Though it had nothing to do with the

50

business she operated, my behavior contained an element of deception. If not toward Mrs. Reisner, certainly toward Gil Dawson. I sank miserably onto my bed and sobbed quietly to myself.

At six o'clock Mrs. Reisner sent word up to us that we were to come to dinner. Helen was conspicuous by her absence when we were all seated. Before dinner was served Mrs. Reisner addressed us sternly.

"Helen is gone and she won't be back. The same thing will happen to the next one who starts a fight."

She gave us to understand by her glance that the matter was closed and that there was to be no further discussion of it. I ate my dinner in silence and without appetite. I felt no sense of vindication. I was sorry for Helen. If I had not come to Hawaii her life would have been unharmed. I could not help being weighted with a heavy sense of guilt.

Word traveled back to the house in a few days that Helen was working in a waterfront house. The information dejected me even more. I made no comment when I heard it, but when Mrs. Reisner was not around Betty had something to say.

"Helen had it coming. We were all for you, kid," she told me. "There isn't a girl in the house that hasn't had trouble with Helen. We were all glad to see her go."

"I'm sorry she could not find better work," I said.

"It's what she's fit for. Helen Gray is nothing but a whore," said Betty.

I glanced at her quickly, but she had said it with a straight face. I wondered what she deluded herself into thinking she was, or any of the rest of us? Our jobs and Helen's were the same. The only difference was in the pay and the surroundings.

Later I learned that Helen had not helped herself when Mrs. Reisner had confronted her in the office. She had been arrogant and defiant as she sought to put all

51

of the blame on me. She even accused Mrs. Reisner of bad judgment when she hired me. It didn't make me feel any better, but I was able to reason that Helen's problem was one of personality—that her complaint against me and the other girls was not well-founded. She was to be pitied. I tried not to think about her any more.

One afternoon, a month later, I was at the beach with Gil. After an hour of swimming, we started for his apartment and encountered Audrey who had been with friends on the beach in front of the Royal. The three of us walked home together and Audrey invited us in to her apartment. A customer had left an unopened bottle with her last night and she saw no reason why we couldn't enjoy it together.

We had a drink, then Gil and I went next door to his apartment. I lived for the carefree, happy moments we were alone together. I had learned to cherish them and not think about the consequences. The fulfillment of being wanted and loved was all any girl could ask, and especially one in my profession where my body was all that counted. Gil loved me for what he thought I was. I knew there would be an end to that someday, when he learned the truth. I guess I was storing those moments up in my memory, to live on for the rest of my life.

"Hey, in there. Are you decent? I've got to see Kimiko at once!" Audrey called as she pounded on the door.

"What's the matter?" asked Gil.

"I've got to talk with Kimiko." Audrey sounded upset and nervous. I walked to the door.

"What do you want, Audrey?"

"I've got to talk with you alone. Step over to my apartment right away."

"Anything that concerns her, concerns me too," Gil announced.

52

"Nothing doing, fellow. You stay right here," Audrey insisted.

"Maybe I'd better go with her," I said. The girl sounded quite disturbed. Maybe she was in trouble.

I left Gil standing in the doorway and accompanied Audrey into her apartment. The Chinese girl turned and faced me, hands on hips. I stared at her wonderingly. I couldn't imagine what was on her mind.

"Why didn't you tell me you worked for Evaline Reisner?" said Audrey in a muffled voice.

I took a step back, stunned by her words. I glanced fearfully over my shoulder, half expecting Gil to be standing outside, listening to what was said.

"How—how did you find out?"

"She was here, only a few moments ago. Didn't you hear the commotion?"

"No." I could hardly believe my ears.

"She said she happened to be driving along Kalakauha when we came home from the beach. She saw us and followed us here. She asked the janitor whose apartment this was, when you and Gil were in here with me having a drink. She knows me, knows what I do around the beach. Then she saw you and Gil go into his apartment. She thinks I arranged it and that you're working for me on the side."

"You told her that was not so?" I groaned.

"Of course I did," Audrey replied. "She didn't believe me, and why should she? Who would ever believe that a gal who works as you and I do, would be carrying on a non-commercial affair?"

"I must get there at once, convince her—"

"Save your energy, kid. You're through. Evaline said she had heard an accusation against you, that you were doing just that! You've already been fired."

"What do you mean?" Audrey seemed to be heaping one calamity after another upon me.

53

"The Madam is sending your clothes and final pay. She said for you not to come back to the house. You're through there. She asked me to tell you that," said Audrey.

I sank into a chair and stared bitterly into space. My world was falling apart, just as it had a few months ago in Tokyo. I should have been used to such upheavals by now, but I wasn't. Each one was a bit harder to swallow. I wondered if there would ever be any security for me? I looked at Audrey. A thin smile crossed her lips.

"You know something, kid? I had you figured right from the start, only I didn't know where you worked," she said. Audrey lit a cigarette and blew a cloud of smoke into the room.

"It's too bad you didn't expose me. It would have been better if you had. It would have saved all of this," I gestured toward Gil's apartment.

As I sat there gazing dismally into the future, Gil came to the door. Audrey was unable to keep him away any longer.

"You've had time enough to talk. Now tell me what this is all about," he said, looking at both of us.

All at once I felt sick.

CHAPTER EIGHT

The room grew heavy with silence. I had the feeling that life had me clutched in an impasse from which there was no escape. I believe Japanese are thought of as a stoic race of people. When Fate overtakes us we assume the posture of Buddha with a bowed head. It does no good to rant and rave at such times. Prayer in any faith is the only solution.

To my surprise it was Audrey Ching who moved in to dominate the moment. That girl, whose `lovely Oriental face and figure contained an Occidental mind and heart, was quick to sense the strife that swirled about Gil and me. And she did not hesitate to take charge.

"Look, Gil. I've got no dinner engagement tonight. Kimiko has just said she can stay here longer than usual. Why don't you go out and get us something to eat? We can fix it right here. Wouldn't that be fun?" She smiled at him.

"Sure it would. But I want to know what's the matter," he insisted.

"Run along and attend to the food. By the time you come back, maybe Kimiko will be able to talk."

"Are you in trouble, honey?" he asked, turning to me.

I looked up at him. My heart nearly burst at the loving concern I saw in his eyes. "I'm all right."

Audrey pushed Gil out of the apartment. "Get going

and don't come back with any two-bit hamburgers either."

Audrey sat down opposite me. She held out a pack of cigarettes. I took one, for I had gradually begun to form western habits. She studied me carefully.

"How do you feel about him?" she asked.

"I like him very much."

"You know he's in love with you."

"Yes, I'm afraid so. I shouldn't have let it happen, but I couldn't help it. I knew all along that it would bring nothing but sorrow to us both."

"The point is, what are you going to do now?"

"I don't know."

"You could marry him if you want to. I'm sure of that," said Audrey.

"He'd leave me the minute he found out the truth. I respect him too much for that." I shook my head dispiritedly. "No. It's over between us. I must tell him the truth now."

"At least wait until after dinner. Let him enjoy his food," Audrey suggested.

I looked at her and agreed with my eyes. "Did you say that Mrs. Reisner was sending my things here?"

"Yes."

"I'm sorry. You oughtn't to be put to such bother."

"It's no trouble for me," said Audrey. "In fact, I've been thinking." She looked at me steadily. "It's damned hard to make ends meet, living alone in a place like this. You're welcome to bunk with me for awhile, providing you'll pay half."

"Thanks much, Audrey. But I'd better not. I'll try for work in one of the other houses." It was all I knew to do.

"Don't be a fool. Reisner's place is okay. But the others are just dumps. You'll work for peanuts."

"At least I would be paying my way."

"Have you got any money?" asked Audrey.

56

"Yes. If Mrs. Reisner sends me all I've got coming, it will be close to five hundred dollars."

Audrey's eyes widened. A broad grin crossed her round, tanned face. Her eyebrows went up.

"You've got nothing to worry about!" she exclaimed. "You're a fool to break things off with Gil, but if you insist on doing it, you'll be a lot better off working as a call girl. The money isn't nearly as steady as it is in a house but you can be your own boss. And you meet men who have more money to throw around. Why don't you give it a try?"

We were still talking when Joe arrived with my clothes. He dumped them on Audrey's studio couch and handed me an envelope with my final pay from Mrs. Reisner.

"Sorry it happened to you, Kimiko, but you should have had better sense than to cross the Madam," he said just before he left.

"Please tell her she's wrong about me," I begged.

Joe shrugged and departed.

"You'll have to stay here overnight in any event," said Audrey, eyeing the clothes. "It's too late now for you to make other arrangements."

I was grateful to Audrey for her hospitality. We hung my clothes in the closet with hers and put my underthings away in a chest. Audrey mixed cocktails and had them ready when Gil returned. He came in with two large paper sacks filled with food.

"After lugging this stuff here I think I'm entitled to an explanation of what the two of you are up to," said Gil.

"You can have a drink before dinner but that's all," Audrey told him gaily.

I would have confessed everything to Gil and had it over with, but I heeded Audrey's advice to wait until after dinner. It would be better to talk with him alone.

57

While Audrey was a close and understanding friend, Gil might resent her presence while learning the truth about me.

We had several rounds of cocktails. Now that I was no longer under Mrs. Reisner's restraint, I did not stop with one. I had never trusted sake or any other strong drink, but the evening loomed forebodingly ahead and I found that it gave me courage.

Gil's spirit improved as he drank. To him the fact that I had remained beyond the afternoon was a major event in our relationship. He took it as a good omen. Before long the drinks make him happy and gay.

"Let's eat," Audrey suggested an hour later. "I've got a date later on and I'll leave you both to do the dishes."

We cleared the small table in the living room and set it with plastic plates. Gil had brought steaks with French fried potatoes and tossed salad. He went to his own kitchen and came back with cold beer. As we ate I kept wondering how to tell him. My worry disappeared for a while as we relaxed over coffee and cigarettes. It was pleasant to be here with these kind people in this small, friendly room at Waikiki. By now Betty and the others at Mrs. Reisner's would be preparing themselves for the impersonal desire of strangers.

Gil and I were still sitting at the table when Audrey changed to go on her date. She appeared in a colorful sarong-like dress and high heels. Gil gave her a low, appreciative whistle.

"I pity the fellow you're after tonight," he said, in a kidding way.

"Don't worry about him. He'll get his money's worth." She glanced at me before she went out. "Look after things, Kimiko. I'll be back around midnight."

When we were alone, Gil turned surprised and questioning eyes on me.

58

"She sounded as if you were staying here all night."

"I am."

I had to acquaint him with the facts sooner or later. I saw the perplexed look in his eyes. Now was as good a time as any.

"But she's—" Gil stopped. "Don't get me wrong, Kimi. I like Audrey a lot. She isn't your kind of girl, though. She's different, and I think you know what I mean. Why are you staying here instead of going home?"

"I have no home, Gil. You might as well know." An overwhelming sadness descended upon me as I said it.

"Honey, why didn't you say this before?" he asked, after a long silence.

He took me in his arms. We had moved over to the couch to finish our coffee. I let him kiss me, then pushed him away. Our eyes held for a moment, then I drew a deep breath.

"I have been awfully wrong in the way I've let you go on believing in me, Gil."

"Believing in you! That's not the half of it. I love you, Kimiko."

"You won't when I've finished talking."

I stood up. It was no good sitting close to him. His nearness distracted me. I had to get hold of myself. No man had ever given me this helpless feeling. It was a bad thing I had to do to him. I hated it, but I could no longer permit my heart to rule my head. He looked at me with perplexity.

"I don't get it," he said.

"I'm like Audrey. If anything, I'm worse, as American men view such things. You have been kind and good to me. I let you because I've always longed for respect. It was a mistake from the beginning."

Gil started to arise from the couch. "But—"

"No. Stay where you are, Gil. Let me finish." I gave him a hard smile. "I never intended seeing you again

59

after that first time, but I couldn't help myself. But now you must know. I'm another Audrey Ching. In Japan I was a geisha. When I came to Hawaii I went to work for Mrs. Reisner who runs a house in the valley."

"Reisner?" Gil echoed the name, his face blank.

"You know her? You know of her place?"

"I've heard of it. You didn't come from there. No!" he protested.

"It's true, Gil. From the time I was old enough, I have catered to men's whims and desires."

He leaped to his feet. "Kimiko! You're out of your mind! Why are you saying such a thing? Tell me who you are?"

"I have told you."

"But it's not the truth." He grabbed my arms and spun me around to face him. "You want to discourage me. Well, you won't! You can't get rid of me that way." His brow darkened.

I was aghast that he refused to believe me. What could I do to make him face facts? I pushed him away.

"I'm telling you this for your own good, Gil. You must not love me. Girls in my work are to be used only for pleasure."

"You're lying!"

"No. It's the truth!" I cried.

But he was not prepared to accept the story. He suspected that I had made it up for reasons yet unexplained. His face was a mask of exasperation. Suddenly he went to the kitchen and came back with a bottle. He poured two drinks and handed me one.

"Drink it. Maybe it will jolt you back to your senses," he ordered.

"I know exactly what I am saying," I pleaded.

"Why do you want to be rid of me?"

"I don't, Gil—I mean," I added hastily, "you've got to know the truth about me. And it's what I said."

60

He brooded over that for a long time. Then he said, "Don't ever say that again."

I looked at him helplessly. There was nothing more I could do. In time, I grew uncomfortable under his gaze and began to clear the table. Later, when the dishes were dried and put away I joined him in the living room. He had drunk considerable whiskey.

"I won't let you stay with Audrey," he announced all of a sudden.

"But I've got to sleep somewhere."

"It won't be here. Come on." Gil lunged out of his chair. He had drunk so much, so rapidly, that he was unsteady on his feet.

It wasn't until I discovered that he merely wanted me to go to his apartment instead of remaining in Audrey's that I consented to budge from the room. We went next door. Inside he turned to me.

"I ought to be sore as hell at you for telling me that wild tale but I'm not," he said, taking me in his arms and holding me possessively.

"Don't make it worse, Gil."

His hands traveled over me. I felt a response to the yearning of his body. I debated what to do. Gil was going to feel terrible in the morning from the whiskey he had drunk. Maybe it was just as well that he awake to complete reality.

"I'm going to make it better," he smiled. "I want you, Kimiko."

"All right." I gave in. "But make us some more drinks first."

I was stalling for time. I had made up my mind what to do. While he was in the kitchen I removed my dress. If I could not convince him one way, perhaps another way would do the trick. I knew of no better way than to exhibit the technique of the courtesan.

61

When he returned with the drinks I stood naked before him, smiling without shame.

"I hope you'll be pleased tonight, sweetheart," I said softly.

Gil swayed on his feet as he looked at me. I pressed against him and took one of the drinks from his hand. I parted my lips and lifted them to his. He almost emptied his glass with one gulp, then staggered to the couch with me. I leaned back on my outstretched arms, displaying my body for his enjoyment.

He touched me with his hands, then his arms encircled my waist. I lay back, drawing him down upon me. I fought a sudden and terrific need for him. His passion was almost more than I could bear and for one wild second my defense almost crumbled. But that was a luxury I could not afford. I could never fall in love again as I had with Gil. I knew it now and admitted it to myself. I was acting a part, one I knew so well. And I was not through with him yet. Not until I had turned his passion into hatred could I complete my service to the man I loved.

"Gil, darling, you're not tired," I murmured in his ear a long time later. "You must not let this night go with such a short-lived pleasure."

He mumbled drunkenly and stared at me. I smiled and stroked his fevered forehead.

"You must find new excitement with me," I said. "What would please you?"

It took him a moment to figure out what I was saying. The storm had passed. All he wanted now was sleep. He closed his eyes and rested against me.

"No. Your time with me is limited. Make the most of it, Gil," I urged. I almost despaired of going through with this, but I forced back my anguish. It would never do to try and salvage anything between us. I had to kill it. Tonight! I went on. "Say what you want of me. Anything. I'll do anything you say."

"What?" He stared at me, vaguely incredulous.

"Yes, lover," I said soothingly. "My life is yours while you're with me. Your pleasure is my wish."

Gil raised a trembling hand to his head. His eyes stared at me strangely, as if comprehending at last. I saw the torment in his face and almost cried out my love for him. Why did I have to make him suffer like this? At that instant I nearly gave in to my despair.

But then, suddenly, Gil's eyes went blank. He fell back on the couch in utter oblivion. I knelt by his side and my heart thumped painfully. When I was sure he had passed out I stood up. I bit my lips to keep them from trembling.

In a moment I was into my clothes. I crossed through the darkness of the court back to Audrey's apartment.

CHAPTER NINE

My nerves were taut as I paced the floor of the apartment. The evening with Gil had not been long, but it had shattered my emotions. Audrey was due back, for it was after midnight. She knew American men. She would know if I had handled Gil properly. I needed her advice and her assurance. I was so upset that I could not think straight.

My life in Japan had never been complicated like this. I had never known the anguish of the heart. It was a new kind of torture, and I knew of no nostrums or panaceas that could cure it. Audrey came in at one o'clock.

"How did things go with you and Gil?" she asked, getting out of her clothes.

"I told him about my work but he wouldn't believe it."

"That doesn't surprise me. Gil is a bit of an idealist. Where is he now?"

"Next door. Dead drunk."

"Life will hit in the face in the morning," Audrey predicted with a mirthless smile. She got into a pongee jacket that hung just below her bare hips. "Speaking of drinks, how about a nightcap? You look as if you could use one."

I said nothing. Audrey went into the kitchen and came back with two highballs. She handed me a glass

64

then sat down and stretched her legs out in front of her.

"The guy I was with tonight didn't drink. Can you imagine that?" Audrey smiled. She took a long pull at her highball. "Getting back to Gil. He's a good friend and neighbor and I hate to see him shook up. But I could see it building up from the moment he met you."

"It was all my fault," I admitted.

"Right. But you made him happy for a while. You got him over the girl back home and that's worth something. Did he ever tell you about her?"

I looked at her questioningly.

"He mooned to me about her for the first month that he lived here. She didn't sound very interesting, but Gil goes all out. When he falls in love, it's with both feet. He'll get over you too, but it might take a little longer," she said.

"You sound awfully sure of what you say, Audrey."

"It's as good a guess as any. American boys are funny. In the Islands we don't take things nearly as seriously as they do on the mainland. I don't know how it is where you came from."

"Where I came from love can be quite beautiful. Japanese stories are filled with such tragedies, so sad but so touching. They are for others, though. A geisha does not let herself become involved."

Audrey looked at me with surprise. "Then why are you worried about Gil?"

"I have never been involved before. He is the first man I have ever really loved."

"Don't you want him to get over you?" Audrey asked.

"Yes, I do. We could never be married. I am no good for him."

The Chinese girl gazed at me for a long moment, then slowly shook her head. I had the notion that she was puzzled by my remark but I did not know how to explain it.

"It looks to me as if you've got to do some forgetting yourself. You'll have to if you live with me, because you have your share of the rent to pay."

"I can't stay here, Audrey."

"Suit yourself about that. But I've already made a date for you for tomorrow night. That's if you want it. You'll make fifty bucks. A fellow I know is entertaining a friend from Los Angeles. He asked if I could get a girl for his friend and I said yes, having you in mind. How about it?"

Audrey Ching had befriended me and now she was offering me a chance to earn my way. I knew I should make the effort while I was with her. It was the least I could do to show my appreciation.

"Yes. I'll go along."

"Good. We'd better get some shut-eye. If your date is anything like mine, tomorrow night will be a long one." Audrey finished her drink.

The studio couch in Audrey's apartment opened into a double bed. We did not bother with covers for the night was warm. Audrey was asleep the instant her head hit the pillow. It was a full hour later when I dropped off into a troubled slumber.

A milkman at the rear door awakened me the next morning. Audrey was already up. She took in the milk, bantered with the delivery boy, then returned to the living room yawning. I sat up in bed.

"We'd better get organized. I'll take over the kitchen if you'll look after the front of the apartment," she suggested.

"It's your home. I'll do whatever you wish."

"Half of it is yours, so long as you pay. That's the main thing I'm interested in."

We pitched in. By the time I got the studio couch

made up and folded back together, Audrey had breakfast ready. As we ate, she told me about her work. There were call girls who operated through a procurer in Honolulu and she had tried it for a while. She hadn't been satisfied because she could not keep all of her earnings.

"This way, I maintain a few connections here and there and keep what I make. All I'm ever out is an occasional tip to a bellboy or a waiter or someone around the beach," said Audrey, grinning.

"But how can you be sure of dates?" I asked.

"You can't. That's the risk of being in business for yourself. There's a lot to be said for independence. I'm not particular. I've slept with all sorts of men. Still, it's nice to be able to say 'no'."

I couldn't help liking Audrey Ching. She was jaunty and confident and gay. Not many Japanese girls ever achieved her feeling of fun and freedom. I wished I could be like her. She seemed to have found the answer to life, even though someday she would know sorrow, when she was old and ugly and no longer desirable to men. She did not think of that, nor did I. We could not let ourselves think of many tomorrows.

We were drinking the second cup of coffee when we heard Gil stirring about in his apartment. I immediately grew concerned, but Audrey only smiled.

"Why don't you ask him over for a cup of coffee?" she suggested.

"I doubt if he ever wants to see me again."

"That's the way you want him to feel, isn't it?"

"Yes." But deep in my heart I knew that was not so.

"He can hardly avoid seeing you, living right next door. My idea would be to square him away completely. Face facts. That's the way to do it. The quicker people understand the truth, the better off they are."

After that little speech, Audrey didn't wait for me

to comment. She walked to the kitchen door and called to Gil.

"Hey, fellow. Come on over for a spot of coffee."

Gil came through the kitchen door a few minutes later. His eyes were bloodshot and his shoulders sagged. He stopped short when he saw me. His words seemed to come from some dark, brooding recess of his mind.

"I thought perhaps you had gone away, Kimiko."

I looked at him. I wished desperately for some way to comfort him, to do away with the hurt that I saw in his eyes. But there was nothing for me to say.

"She's living with me. We told you that yesterday," said Audrey. "Sit down. You look as if you had tied one on last night."

"I did that, all right," said Gil mournfully.

Audrey gave him a cup of coffee, sat down, lit a cigarette then glanced at Gil brightly. "The reason Kimiko is living with me is strictly business, Gil. You'd better get that straight, if it didn't sink in last night."

He looked at her. Slowly his eyes traveled to me. I lowered my head, avoiding his gaze.

"I was in hopes that I would wake up this morning and discover that it was all a bad dream," he said quietly.

There was a short, painful silence. It was broken by Audrey who launched into some vapid chatter about the beach. She was going surfboard riding with a friend later in the morning. And this afternoon there was to be a hula festival in Kapiolani Park. Listening to her was like hearing the voice of Hawaii—eternally playful, eternally young.

Gil and I were silent. He spoke to me softly, just before he went back to his apartment. Audrey was in the kitchen humming to herself as we faced each other.

"I guess I'll see you around." His tone was bitter.

68

"Yes, Gil. For a while. I'm not sure how long I'll stay with Audrey."

He went out. I watched him until he disappeared through the screen door to his rooms. I stared at the bright sunny morning. The salt air was laden with the scent of hibiscus and frangipanni. Hawaiian music came from a record player across the court. My senses were numb to these pleasant surroundings. I felt nothing but an overpowering sense of loss.

Audrey had her own plans for the day. She told me that she would be back by five o'clock. We were to be dressed by seven and meet our dates at a restaurant on Kalakaua Avenue.

At eleven that morning I put on swim trunks and a bra and hung an aloha shirt loosely about my shoulders. I went to the beach, avoiding the area by the seawall where Gil and I had met. Instead I went to the section between the Outrigger Club and the Moana Hotel.

I removed the shirt and lay prone in the sand, folding my arms for a pillow. The warm sun felt good on my body. I rested, motionless. My mind ached with the tragedy of Gil Dawson but I tried resolutely not to think about anything. In time my world narrowed to nothing but the grains of sand immediately before my eyes. I felt drowsy but did not sleep. My worries were shadows hovering just outside of consciousness. It was good to be stretched out on the sand, in a little world of my own where nothing mattered. Nothing at all. Finally I dozed.

When my mind grew wakeful and I became aware of the surf, of voices and laughter, I rolled over and sat up, brushing the sand from my chest. When my eyes became accustomed to the brightness, I looked out at the Pacific Ocean. White clouds floated on the far horizon, like misty animals. In time my attention came back to the beach. I watched the surfriders and a party going out in a brightly colored outrigger. People played all up and down the beach, as far as I could see. Golden tanned bodies lolled on the sand. I thought that this beach was one of the most famous in the world and that people who played here had money, prestige, position. It was good to be here, thinking only of unimportant things.

It was mid-afternoon before I wearied of the sun. I had remained on the beach through the lunch hour, for I had no appetite. When I left the sand, I sauntered along Kalakaua Avenue looking into shop windows and enjoying my newly found leisure. There was no urgency today to return to the house in the Nuuanu Valley in time for dinner with Mrs. Reisner and the other girls. I was on my own.

If things worked out with Audrey, it could be that I would find some happiness in my new life. I still felt some security because of the money I had saved. But that could disappear overnight, as I well knew. However, if I found fairly steady work, the future might hold even greater promise. If I didn't, there was always River Street.

At the apartment, a short while later, I took a shower. Afterward, I intended taking an inventory of my wardrobe. The garments I had worn at Mrs. Reisner's might not be entirely appropriate for the variety of occasions I would have to face as a party girl at Waikiki. But after I had toweled myself the studio couch looked so inviting that I decided to rest for a few minutes.

"Wake up, Kimiko! We've got to get a move on."

Audrey's voice pulled me out of a deep slumber. I sat up, blinking, instantly aware that the afternoon was gone. It was nearly six. Audrey was busily engaged in throwing off her things so she could take a quick shower before dressing.

"I must have been worn out. All I've done today is rest," I commented as I got off of the couch.

"You might be glad you did before this night is over," Audrey observed merrily.

"What do we wear? I've got an evening dress and—"

"Get your things out. I'll look 'em over."

I showed Audrey what I had.

"They're pretty fancy for the sort of dates we have tonight. But the cocktail dress will do. Tomorrow you'd better buy yourself a simple dress or two," said Audrey before she disappeared into the shower.

We spent the next hour getting ready. Audrey wore a glazed cotton sarong and bolero of lovely Polynesian blue. She was beautiful. She looked at me and nodded approvingly.

"All set?"

"Yes," I told her.

The shadows of night were falling rapidly when we left the apartment. I glanced involuntarily toward Gil's unit as we crossed the court. It was dark inside but his door was open. I wondered if he was watching. I had never felt any guilt at keeping an appointment. But now I hurried along, hoping that Gil would not see me.

We arrived a few minutes later at a restaurant with red checkered tablecloths and hurricane lamps. The lobby was decorated in a nautical manner, with portholes for windows and a ship's rail for the wainscot. A bar extended along one side. Two men left the bar when we walked in. Audrey gave one of them a brilliant smile. His name was George Linton. He was introduced to me. Then I turned to the other man and, because it was my work to please him tonight, I smiled as I was introduced to Walton Creet.

"What a pleasure this is!" he exclaimed. "I have always wanted a date with a Japanese girl!"

71

This man, Walton Creet, puzzled me. He was thirty-eight years old, tall and slender, with dark, thinning hair and a confident voice. He told me that he was a motion picture producer in Hollywood where he enjoyed an immense fortune created by his uncle and since enhanced by his own luck and business acumen. He said he was restless and that three wives had divorced him and four times that many mistresses had given him up as a bad bet. All of this he told me with such casualness and good cheer that it did not sound offensive.

Both men proved to be good dinner companions as we ate lobster in the restaurant at Waikiki. I was hungry, having had nothing to eat since breakfast. Both George and Walton showed great interest when they learned that I had been a geisha in Tokyo. They asked me many questions about my life in that profession.

After dinner we drove across the Pali to windward Oahu, arriving at ten o'clock at George's beach house near Kaneohe. It was a secluded little cottage amid palm trees and looked out over the beach and the booming surf beyond. The men wanted to go swimming.

"What'll we do? We should have brought our suits," I whispered to Audrey when we were alone for a moment.

"They wouldn't let us wear them if we had. I've been here with George before. There's no one within a quarter of a mile and, anyway, it's fun to swim naked."

It was not my idea of fun, as it turned out. It was too cold and the breakers on this side of the island were too wild and stormy. Within ten minutes my teeth were chattering and I appealed to Walton to take me out of this world of water and blowing spume. He was happy to oblige.

The men had brought blankets to the beach. Walton picked up one of them and wrapped it around me and himself. I was so chilled that I rubbed against him for warmth. He embraced me with his arms while I shivered from the cold. Evidently he interpreted my response as an unusually fiery passion when it was nothing more than my escape from the icy water. He held me hungrily and bruised my lips with his.

We lay together on the beach for nearly an hour. I had become warm and comfortable and was content to look up at the billions of stars in the blue-black Hawaiian night, while accommodating Walton's tempestuous desires. Audrey and George were off down the beach somewhere huddled in a blanket of their own.

"You're glorious," Walton breathed in my ear as he rested. "I feel cheated because I didn't meet you until the last night of my stay in Hawaii."

"You're going home tomorrow?" I asked lazily.

"Yes. Damn it. But I'll be back."

"I hope so." I made my voice warm and inviting for that was what men wanted to hear.

At two o'clock the four of us gathered in the kitchen of George's cottage for bacon and eggs and more drinks. Audrey entertained on the lanai with an impromptu hula while George played the ukulele. To please Walton, I drank a lot more than I wanted. I could not understand his insistence that I drink with

73

him. A woman is no good for a man when she is drunk. But it was his money, so I went along. Audrey didn't hold back. She told me that it was the thing to do.

Somewhere during the darkened hours of the morning, time ceased to exist for me. Walton fondled me, Audrey danced and sang risque Hawaiian songs, and George played the ukulele interminably. The liquor had dulled my senses so that everything was out of focus. The antics of my companions seemed to transpire in slow motion before my eyes. One instant, Walton's face loomed large and grinning before me, and the next I knew, he'd be in the kitchen which seemed miles off in the distance. I had the notion that life would go on this way indefinitely. But it didn't.

I awoke suddenly to a rocky world. My mouth felt as if it were filled with the ashes of burnt matches. My eyes ached painfully. I sat up and groaned as every muscle in my body gave protest. For a second I stared around in alarm, not knowing where I was. The room was filled with the pale light of early dawn. Slowly it came to me that this was the bedroom of George's cottage.

To my amazement I was alone in the bed. All thoughts left me just then, except the need for getting to a faucet and drinking gallons of cold water. As I started for the bath room I stumbled over Walton who lay outstretched on the floor. I stared down at him with horror, thinking he might be dead. My parched body needed water before I could go for help. I hurried to the bathroom.

I returned and bent over Walton and discovered that he was not dead at all. He was simply sleeping off the effects of too much liquor. But it worried me that he was on the floor. I tried to lift him to the bed. His limp body was too much for me. I went in search of help. Audrey was asleep on the couch in the living room. I woke her up.

"Where's George? I need him to help get Walton into bed," I told her.

"I don't know," said Audrey sleepily. "What'd you say Walton's trouble was?"

"He's asleep on the floor in the bedroom."

"What's wrong with that?"

"But—" I looked at her in astonishment. "It's not what he's paying me for. He might feel cheated."

"Forget it." Audrey sat up stiffly and glanced at her wristwatch. "The last thing George told me was that we'd all have to get up and out of here early this morning. He's got to put Walton on a plane."

"In his condition? Impossible!" I exclaimed.

"Let George worry about that."

Audrey left the couch and started looking for George. She found him in a hammock outside under a palm tree. She woke him and a moment later they came into the living room. George rubbed his head and smiled blearily at me.

"Quite a party, wasn't it?" he said hollowly.

"I'm afraid your friend might not have enjoyed himself too much. He's in there, asleep on the floor." I pointed to the bedroom.

George laughed. "Don't worry about him. He had the time of his life. If I didn't know he had some important business back in Los Angeles, I wouldn't bother putting him on the plane this morning. But I guess you kids would like to get home."

To my surprise George went to a desk and came back with a handful of money. He gave it to Audrey.

"It's the usual and a tip for each of you besides. You'd better take a taxi across the island. I won't have time to take you home. I've got to sober up Walton and get him to the airport," he said.

Audrey and I dressed. We had to wait half an hour for a taxi to come out from Kanehoe to pick us up.

Audrey counted the money and handed half of it to me. We each had a hundred dollars plus a ten-dollar tip.

"I don't know why they got so drunk when they came in from the beach. I'm sure it spoiled their fun," I commented.

"They got their money's worth," said Audrey yawning.

"Are all the parties you go on like this?"

"A lot of them."

I wondered what I had let myself in for. Spending the night with a man was one thing, but having to get drunk with him was something entirely different. It was not the proper way to earn money. I was still thinking about that when the taxi arrived.

Business men, office workers, clerks and stenographers were already on their way to work in the trade marts of Honolulu when we arrived home that morning. Our work day was done and we were tired. I was half sick from the liquor I had drunk. Within ten minutes both of us were in bed asleep, the Venetian blind on the east window adjusted to keep out the bright, warm sunshine.

The noon hour was past when I awoke. Instead of getting up I lay contemplating the ceiling, my mind reviewing the events of last night. Hiring out as a drinking partner was something I was not accustomed to. Girls who did that could not last long. It aged them too rapidly. If last night was typical of the sort of business Audrey conducted, I did not think that I would be happy with her. But one night was not necessarily a fair test. After thinking it over I decided I would try it a while longer. It might take several weeks to see the pattern of things.

I was in the kitchen measuring coffee into the perco-

76

lator when Audrey joined me. She rubbed the sleep out of her eyes and smiled.

"Some party, wasn't it?" she said.

"If you like drinking, it was."

I poured two cups of coffee and we sat down.

"What have you got against a little sip now and then? Don't they do any drinking in Tokyo?" Audrey asked.

"Oh yes, but the object is to enjoy it. I still feel sorry for Walton Creet, having to catch a plane this morning. I wonder if he made it."

"If he didn't, we'll see more of him. You went over big. And that fellow has money. He'd be a good one for you to latch onto."

I drank my coffee. He had said he would come back, but I never put much faith in words. Many men had told me that, and some had returned. But as a rule I never saw them again. With the exception of Gil, I had never met a man whom I longed to see again, save for the money he was willing to spend. I felt that way about Walton Creet. He was just another customer—and a drunken one at that.

"What have you arranged for tonight?" I asked.

"It's still open," Audrey replied.

"Open and no prospects?" I glanced at her with surprise.

Audrey shook her head. "But don't worry. I might get a call toward evening. If I do, I'll try and work you in also."

I didn't like such a haphazard arrangement. I did not comment on it, however. Again I thought it best to wait and see how things worked out. Give it a fair trial.

Late that afternoon Audrey took me shopping. I bought some clothes that were more fitting for my new needs. I was horrified at the prices. The expedition set me back nearly a hundred dollars. But, according to Audrey, I was now ready for any sort of an occasion.

77

There was no sign of Gil when we returned to the apartment for dinner. His front door was shut tight. It was not until the following day that I learned from the caretaker that he had gone to Hilo and might not return for a week.

It was during that time that I received my indoctrination into Audrey Ching's way of life. The girl worked through no established contacts. When she awakened in the morning or afternoon she seldom knew where her next dollar was coming from. It was frightening.

But at that, the first week was profitable. Audrey arranged two more dates for me. I spent an evening with a man on his cabin cruiser in the Ala Wai. Two nights later I slept in a hotel room. My third date was a pick-up from the beach. Audrey had warned me that I must be extremely careful about entertaining men at the apartment. The pick-up did not start out as a date at all.

He was an American who struck up an acquaintance with me as I lay sunning myself on the sand. He was pleasant enough and persuaded me to have dinner with him. He called for me at the apartment after I had dressed. Later, when he made known his desire for me, I caused him some astonishment by quoting him a price and suggesting that we retire to his hotel room. He had qualms about that so I took him to the apartment, knowing that Audrey would not be home until morning.

We talked for a long time, for he was greatly interested in my stories about Japan. It was one o'clock when he finally left. I walked to the door with him, wearing a short Mandarin jacket. He kissed me, then departed as a taxi pulled up in front of the court. He hailed the driver as the other fare was making change.

I turned back into the room and picked up the dollar bills he had left on the table. I heard footsteps in

78

the court but paid no attention as I counted the money. The footsteps came to a sudden halt. I looked out into the darkness of the court but could not see who it was.

A few moments later I heard Gil let himself into his apartment. He slammed the door shut behind him. I rushed to the window and looked out, knowing that he had returned. I saw the square of light from his apartment reflected on the grass. Then I heard movement in his apartment.

The footsteps outside had been his. He must have seen my visitor leave, and he must have watched me count the money I had earned with my body.

Regret overtook me and I wanted desperately to go to him. But I knew I didn't dare.

CHAPTER ELEVEN

"Maybe he's sick."

Audrey voiced the fear that had been growing in me for two days. The morning after Gil's return, we had heard him moving about in his apartment. But all that afternoon and evening he had been quiet. We heard him again, but briefly, the second day. And now, in the late afternoon, when we returned home after a swim, Gil's apartment was ominously silent.

"Do you think he is?" I asked.

"We'll soon find out."

Audrey went out the back door and called to Gil. I waited, harkening to his answer. When none came, Audrey tried the screen. It was unlocked. She disappeared into his apartment. I waited nervously. Audrey was gone for ten minutes. The moment she appeared I knew something was wrong.

"He's got a fever, but he refused to let me call a doctor," she said.

"Has he been sick long, did he say?"

"He said he hadn't been feeling well when he returned from Hilo. He went up in the mountains and caught a cold. But he said he'd drink some tea if I'd bring it to him," Audrey replied.

"I'll make it for him."

I put a pan of water on to boil, prepared a cup and saucer and a lemon. I was grateful that I could do this little thing for him. Part of the responsibility for Gil's illness was mine. Had I been a different sort of girl, I could have given him happiness. I wished I might deliver the tea to him, but he had asked Audrey. If I went in her place it might serve only to upset him more.

I had a date that night which would keep me occupied until morning but Audrey thought she would be home shortly after midnight.

"Look in on him, will you?" I asked the Chinese girl. "When I get home in the morning, I'll prepare his breakfast."

Audrey gave me a sly smile. "You've got it bad for him, haven't you?"

"I can be kind to him. I only wish I could do more."

My date was with an Australian who had come to Honolulu on business. To my dismay, he insisted on doing the town. I spent the evening masquerading my concern for Gil with a superficial gaiety. We danced in a night club for a while, then went on to visit several bars in the city and at Waikiki. Toward the end he grew maudlin as we sat in a booth drinking Scotch.

"I say, you're an exquisite little Jap. It's a bloody shame you have to earn your money this way," he expostulated.

"But I haven't earned it yet." I wished he would let me so I could be rid of him.

"You will." Suddenly he leered.

"Not if we sit here drinking all night."

"Very well, my dear."

He signaled for the check. In a taxi, riding to his rooms he again reprimanded me for my way of life. I tried not to show my impatience. I was afraid he'd be the sort who spent the night pursuing the favors he had unhesitatingly purchased.

He made ardent love to me in his rooms near the beach. I was not impressed. Enough of this nonsense.

81

My fee was not for listening to his talk. As a geisha I would have entertained him with talk as long as he liked. I was amazed at the way I had gotten over that training. All men wanted of me these days was sensual response to their lust. I brought my talents into use and before long he was silent, holding me clasped in his arms.

I slept by his side until six-thirty the next morning. If my services were no longer required I meant to find it out quickly. Gently I awakened him.

"I must go soon," I advised softly.

He stared up at me as if I were a stranger. When wakefulness came to him he tried to brighten, but his head was splitting with a hangover.

"Oh, oh," he groaned, sinking back to the pillow. "I say, old girl, you're most desirable, but I need shut-eye more than anything in the world right now."

"Then I may leave?"

"Do any bloody thing you like, but don't bother me!" He rolled over and went back to sleep.

I hurried into my clothes. I let myself out, pulling the door shut softly behind me. No cabs were in sight when I reached the street, and rather than wait I struck out for home on foot. Audrey opened her eyes sleepily as I entered the apartment twenty minutes later.

"How is Gil?" I asked immediately.

"Now how should I know that?" She gave me a reproachful glance.

"Didn't you look in on him when you got home last night?"

"The guy I was with kept me out until four o'clock. I couldn't bust in on Gil at that hour, stupid."

I debated a moment. No matter how Gil felt about me, he would surely accept my help if he needed it. I turned abruptly and went next door to his apartment.

"May I come in, Gil?" I called softly.

82

No answer. I tried the door. It was unlocked. I tip-toed in. He was lying on the couch, a lightweight cover drawn up over him. I bent close. His face was pale and had an unhealthy look. I stood undecided for a moment. It was best to let him sleep. I sat down in a chair near the couch and began a vigil that lasted until nearly ten-thirty that morning.

"What can I do for you, Gil?" I asked when he stirred at last.

He gazed at me for a long moment, then looked away. "Nothing. I'll be all right."

"You're sick."

As if to prove me wrong he sat up on the edge of the couch. A moment later he stood up unsteadily and gave me a wan smile.

"You see—" he began, but that's all he said. The next second he collapsed on the couch.

I leaped to him. Nervously I felt his forehead. It was afire. I did what I could to make him comfortable, then ran back to the apartment and shook Audrey out of her sleep.

"Do you know a doctor? We've got to do something for Gil right away."

Audrey grumbled as she sat up. When her thoughts cleared she said, "But Gil doesn't want one. He said so yesterday."

"He's so sick he doesn't know what he's saying," I replied tearfully.

Audrey arose and pulled on a silk Chinese kimono. She went to the telephone. A minute later she was talking to a Dr. Nakama.

"He'll be over in half an hour," said Audrey, turning away from the phone.

I went back to Gil. He lay trembling on the couch. I pulled a blanket over him. There was nothing more I could do but sit down and wait. Audrey came over a few minutes later. We were discussing his condition in quiet tones when the doctor arrived.

Dr. Nakama was an efficient little man of Japanese-American ancestry. He gave us both a slight bow, listened to Audrey's brief explanation of the case, then bent over the patient. He sat on the edge of the couch taking Gil's temperature and pulse, frowning a bit at the results. He adjusted a stethoscope to his ears and listened gravely as he examined Gil's chest.

"It might be a slight touch of pneumonia," the doctor announced a few minutes later. "If his condition doesn't improve today, he should go into a hospital. Who's looking after him?"

"I am," I said.

The doctor nodded. He showed me some medicine and how to administer it. If Gil appeared to be getting worse I was to phone him immediately. Otherwise, he'd be back around five o'clock this afternoon. With that he left.

"He should have sent him to the hospital right away. We're not set up to look after him," said Audrey.

"I can do what's necessary."

"You can't earn money as a nurse," the Chinese girl retorted.

I ignored her and set to work immediately making Gil as comfortable as possible. Audrey looked on for a while, then shrugged and left the apartment.

I remained at Gil's side throughout the day. When Dr. Nakama returned in the late afternoon, he gave Gil another examination and ordered him to the hospital at once.

"There is no use taking any chances," he said. He glanced at me. "Do you have a car?"

"No. I don't even drive," I apologized.

"In that case, if you'll get him into some clothes, I'll drive him."

Gil submitted without protest to the change. He was so sick at this point that he didn't care what happened. I helped him into a shirt and a pair of trousers. Between me and the doctor we managed to get him out to the car, and took him to the hospital in the hills above Honolulu.

I made the necessary arrangements in the hospital office. I assumed financial responsibility for any expense incurred, because I didn't know what else to say when the head nurse asked me about it. I went to the hospital room and stood aside unobtrusively while a nurse and an intern attended to Gil.

"Will he be all right?" I asked, walking out with them when they had finished.

"It depends on whether his fever breaks during the night," the intern told me. He was a young man and he looked me over with interest. "Are you his wife?"

"No."

He smiled, said nothing, then walked off down the long corridor. I didn't know what to do. There was a sitting room at the other end of the hall. A half-dozen people waited there.

I sat down. People glanced my way. I had the odd feeling that I was an intruder. There was nothing more that I could do for Gil. The nurses and the doctors would care for him. Yet, my anxiety over his condition would not permit me to leave. I sat in the room for an hour as people came and went, trying not to be noticed. Once I looked up to see a young man studying my legs. He smiled and winked. I arose and went out.

I knew that I did not belong in Gil's room, yet it was better than sitting outside being stared at by young men. Gil's room was in semi-darkness when I entered. He was asleep. Quietly I took a chair in the corner. I was still sitting there late that night when a nurse came in.

The nurse did not see me at first and was startled when I moved. "What are you doing here? Visiting hours are long over."

"I'm just waiting."

"Are you a relative?"

"No."

"Then you'll have to leave," she said sharply.

"But he has no one," I said.

The nurse deferred any further talk as Gil stirred. His fever was still high and his mind was wandering. He spoke unintelligibly as the nurse gave him her attention. The intern came in to see how he was doing and was not pleased with Gil's progress. Later, I followed the intern out into the corridor.

"Please, if I might I'd like to remain with him."

"There's nothing you can do."

"I only want to know if he will recover."

"If I knew I'd tell you." The intern lowered his voice. "You want to stay with him, don't you?"

I nodded. Indeed I did!

"I can't tell you it's okay to stay here, but if you don't cause any trouble, who will know the difference?" He walked away quickly.

I went back into the room and made myself as unobtrusive as possible in the chair in the corner. The long hours of the night wore on and I prayed for Gil. I dozed. Once I awoke to hear him talking. What he said didn't make sense, but once I was startled out of my wits at the mention of my name. It was early morning when the nurse and intern returned. I had hardly moved in all that time. I watched as they examined Gil.

"The fever is broken," said the intern.

"Does that mean he'll be all right?" I asked.

"Yes." He looked at me thoughtfully. "But I'm afraid you'll be our next patient if you don't get yourself some rest. Your friend is out of danger. You ought to go home and sleep."

I was overwhelmed with gratitude and relief. Gil would grow healthy again and that was all that mattered to me. I rode home in a taxi. Audrey heard me come in and sat up in bed.

"I didn't know you had a job last night," she said.

"It wasn't the kind you think. I was at the hospital with Gil," I told her as I got out of my clothes.

"What? Are you insane?" Audrey exclaimed.

"I only wanted to know that he would get well, and he is."

Audrey watched as I prepared to lie down. My body was stiff and my muscles ached from sitting in the chair all night. I stretched out tiredly. Sleep began to overtake me almost immediately.

"You're the damndest!" Audrey muttered.

I murmured something in Japanese but was too weary to know myself what I had said. The next instant I was fast asleep.

CHAPTER TWELVE

Gil remained in the hospital for a week. I visited him daily and turned down three dates that would have interfered with my trips to the hospital. At first he had little to say to me as I sat in the chair beside his bed. But one morning when I arrived, he was sitting up and smiling. He greeted me as he might a friend whom he was genuinely glad to see.

"You're feeling much better," I observed.

"Yes. It's swell of you to keep coming here, Kimiko. And thanks for those." He nodded toward a bouquet of orchids I had sent.

"They're from Audrey and me both," I told him.

"The intern told me how you sat up with me all through that first night. Why did you do it?"

"Because I was worried."

Gil's recovery, as in most cases of serious illness, had provided him with a more detached viewpoint. Now that he was getting well he was able to consider the daily world he had left for a while. His outlook was better, his attitude more serene.

"You shouldn't have been. I'm not worth it," he grinned.

"In Japan a man is worth a girl's life, if she loves him."

"Isn't Audrey keeping you busy?"

"Not so busy that I can't come to see you."

88

"Why do you feel that way?"

"Just because I do."

I could not explain it. How does any woman explain love when it comes to her? Suddenly it's there, and then, maybe, you think of a lot of little signs that you had known along the way but failed to heed. Suddenly you know it was meant to be this way all along. You belong to that man forever from then on.

"And yet," said Gil, musing, "tonight you will be holding a total stranger, giving him your love."

I glanced at him quickly. Gil was staring philosophically at the bed covering.

"That is not love. There's no connection that I can see," I told him.

"No, I guess you can't." He gave me a kindly smile and sat back against the pillows. "Strange, isn't it?"

"Strange?" I looked at him, frankly puzzled.

Gil laughed. "Don't look so concerned. I'm only kidding. What's really strange to me is the way you and Audrey take life as it comes."

"That's her idea, not mine."

"But from a few of the things she mentioned I figured that you had been in business longer than she."

"I learned to be a geisha. A girl begins early in that training."

"You worked in Mrs. Reisner's house for a while."

"That is true, Gil." I did not want to talk about that.

"Why did you leave?"

"Mrs. Reisner asked me to. She thought I was working elsewhere in the afternoons—the afternoons I used to meet you at the beach."

"What!" He sat forward and stared at me. "Do you mean to say it was my fault?"

I nodded but added quickly, "You were not to blame."

"Well, I'll be damned!" said Gil.

"That's all over now. It doesn't matter any longer.

Someday it may prove to be the right thing, that I did not continue to work there."

"Do you know what I was doing in Hilo?" he asked, abruptly changing the subject.

"No."

"For some time I've been looking around the Islands for a business. I've got some money to invest and want to get something to do. Over there I came across a fellow who owns a gift shop. He's doing well with it, but he's moving to the mainland and there's a chance that I might buy him out."

"That would be nice, living on the big island," I said. I had heard much about the island of Hawaii, so beautiful and big and not built up like Oahu. I wanted to go there, and to the other islands in the Hawaiian archipelago.

Gil talked on. With his recovery was a renewed interest in life. His enthusiasm made me happy. He was full of ideas about what he would do if he bought the gift shop. He had even considered handling some export items on the side, novelties that he could ship back to the United States for sale. I remained with him until the nurse came in and announced that visiting hours were over.

Though I had enjoyed my visit with Gil and was relieved to know that he was recovering, I was slightly disturbed as I rode home on the bus from the hospital. Gil's attitude had changed and I was confused as to what it meant. I had seen the regard for me in his eyes, but not once during my visit that afternoon had he looked at me with longing, as he had on so many other occasions before his sickness. I tried to put those thoughts out of my mind, but they kept nagging at me.

When I reached home, Audrey was seated at the table figuring with pencil and paper.

"How's Gil this afternoon?" she asked, when I walked in.

"Much better. In a few days he expects to be home."

"That's good," she said absently.

Audrey continued to concentrate on the figures. I had a shower and got into a sarong. When I returned to the living room, Audrey was frowning at the accounts that lay on the table before her.

"When you moved in with me I didn't think I'd be worrying about finances. But, damn it, we're getting awfully close to the red ink, and the landlord will be around tomorrow to collect the rent."

"Is that all we owe?" I asked.

"Is that all! That would be enough! But there's more —a whole hell of a lot more! Groceries. The phone bill and the repair work on the ice box!" Audrey broke off and contemplated me. "When you came here we agreed on a fifty-fifty split of all expenses except our personal things, remember?"

"Yes."

"Have you got a hundred and forty-one dollars and sixty cents? That's half of everything we owe at the moment."

"Yes. I can pay that."

I went to the drawer where I kept my money. I took out all I had and counted it. When I paid Audrey I had only thirty-eight dollars left. To date I had paid all of Gil's hospital expenses. In addition, the apartment was expense out of my own purse; an item that I had not worried about at Mrs. Reisner's. For the past week I had worked comparatively little. Until this very moment I hadn't realized my precarious position. My savings were gone. I had little more than I'd had when arriving in Hawaii. Audrey's voice brought me out of this gloomy contemplation.

"And another thing," my roommate was saying. "I

91

can't continue to hustle business for you all the time. You'll have to go after some of it yourself."

"I will, Audrey," I promised, but I did not feel very confident about the results. A geisha girl is not forward with men. She awaits their advances.

"Do you have a date tonight?" Audrey asked.

"No."

"Then you'd better see if you can scare one up. We've got to get some money ahead."

Audrey left the apartment at eight o'clock that evening. She had an engagement that would keep her occupied until the next morning. I had to do what Audrey wanted me to. I could not let her down. I changed into a yellow print dress, gave special care to my make-up and went out.

I walked over to Kalakaua and joined the parade along the sidewalks. It was a balmy evening and the moon was beginning to peek over Diamond Head. Many wealthy vacationers strolled by looking in the expensive shop windows. I sauntered a few blocks, alert for business.

I attracted a few low whistles, but always the male I had attracted proved to be a young fellow unwilling to pay for my favors. Finally a middle-aged man wearing a gaudy aloha shirt smiled at me as I stood looking into a shop window. I glanced at him from the corners of my eyes, then gave him a tentative smile in return. He moved over to me.

"I don't see anything in that window that could make you look any prettier," he said.

"Not even that?" I pointed to a bikini swim suit, hoping to catch his interest. It worked.

"Hummmmm. I take it back," he laughed.

We talked for a few moments. After that I wasted no time. He invited me to have a drink with him. I declined, but offered to give him a drink if he would like to come to my apartment. The man looked surprised, then pleased.

"Where do you live, girlie?"

"Not far from here." I smiled invitingly.

"It's a deal," he announced, taking my arm.

When my visitor was gone an hour later, I put the fifty dollars he had left in the drawer. I repaired my make-up, eyed myself critically in the mirror and set out again.

At eleven o'clock I considered entering one of the bars to see if I could make a pickup. As I stood debating, a man in a light suit and panama hat walked by. He glanced back over his shoulder and I caught his eye. A moment later he returned and stopped in front of me. He was in his late twenties or early thirties, stocky and broad-shouldered.

"Waiting for someone?" he asked.

"You, perhaps," I replied.

"In that event you needn't wait any longer," he smiled.

In less than a minute he had agreed to accompany me to the apartment. I was a little amazed at the ease with which these men agreed to my price. There was no argument. No hesitation. I wondered if I had asked enough.

At the apartment, the man removed his hat and coat. I offered him a drink but he turned it down. He took out his wallet and handed me the money. I pressed against him and patted his cheek.

"We don't need no preliminaries. Just get undressed, baby," he said.

He watched as I removed my dress. His eyes gleamed at my nakedness, but only for an instant. I saw a strange hardness come into them. I smiled and went to the couch. When he did not follow me I looked around. To my amazement he turned and picked up the phone.

"This is Mitchel. Send a car around. We'll be waiting for you on the corner of Kaiulani and Koa," he said when the connection was made.

I gazed at him mystified. He put down the receiver and turned to me. For a second, compassion showed on his face, then he spoke crisply.

"Get your clothes on, kid. You're under arrest."

I did not understand. "What do you mean?"

"Just what I said."

"You don't like me?"

"I'm not being paid to like girls. I don't like what I'm doing any better than you do, but someone has to do it. Hurry up. The patrol car will be around in a few minutes. Get your clothes on and come along," he ordered.

When it got through to me that he represented the police I was both confused and dismayed. I pleaded, "But what have I done wrong?"

"I've often wondered about that question. More than one girl has asked it. Don't you really believe you're doing wrong?"

"If there are rules I don't know about—"

"Look. Just get dressed and come with me. Don't cause any commotion or it'll go harder on you," he said, growing impatient.

I slipped on my clothes. I was nervous as we left the apartment. The officer explained that he did not want to embarrass my neighbors by having a patrol car pull up in front. He led me two blocks away and we waited under a street lamp at a corner. Presently a patrol car arrived. The officer behind the wheel glanced at me curiously. I was put in the seat beside him and the man who had arrested me got in behind.

94

"What's this one been up to, Mitch?" asked the driver as we headed toward Honolulu.

"Hustling along Kalakaua. I spotted her earlier in the evening but couldn't figure that a Jap like her would be pounding the pavements." He addressed a question to me. "Can't you find an easier way to make a living?"

"I'm sorry. I didn't know it was the wrong thing to do," I said.

"If we let you girls work the beach like you were doing tonight the hotels would be empty within a year. What sort of a place do you think Waikiki is?"

"I don't know," I admitted truthfully.

"The least you could have done was to stay west of Fort Street," said the officer dryly.

The night became one of complete confusion to me. I was taken to jail, booked on a charge of vagrancy and locked up in a cell with two other women. One of them was drunk and snored loudly as she lay on a cot. The other was a disheveled, dark-skinned girl who had been in a rumpus involving three sailors and a dice game.

"What's your trouble, friend?" asked the girl, after she had borrowed a cigarette from me.

"I still don't know what I did wrong," I said unhappily. "I entertained a gentleman who turned out to be a police officer. He arrested me and brought me here."

"Where were you working?"

"At Waikiki."

"That's what you did wrong! My gosh! Don't you know any better than that? They don't want streetwalkers around the beach. It'll give the place a bad name. I was in business for a while, but I worked at the Sandman's. It's too risky being around on the street."

Suddenly I understood. It was a matter of location

95

rather than morals. I grew nervous wondering how long they would keep me in the prison.

"What do they do to you when you're arrested?" I asked.

"Is this your first time?"

"Yes."

The girl lowered her voice. "Tell 'em you've never done it before. Maybe they'll let you go."

I lit a cigarette. We smoked in silence as we sat on our cots. The room was chilly, dank and forbidding. A great despondency descended upon me. I had failed to adjust myself to my new life. I had made one mistake after another in Hawaii. Suddenly the girl spoke again.

"I wish this was my first time in. They're liable to ship me out of here."

"Where will they send you?" I asked.

"Maybe back home. That happened just last week to a girl I know. A girl who was doing all right around the island. She used to work in a classy joint up in the Nuuanu Valley."

I was instantly alert. "What was her name?"

"Helen Gray. She got in trouble once too often. They sent her to San Francisco with instructions never to come back."

I thought of Helen as the girl rambled on. I was truly sorry to hear of her misfortune. It was partly my fault. Everyone seemed to have trouble because of me. I began to wonder if I bore a curse, for myself and for others.

We were awakened at six o'clock the next morning, and given a breakfast of coffee and rolls. A police matron appeared and let me out of the cell. In a nearby office I was ordered to remove my clothes. A doctor came in and gave me an examination. When I was dressed again, the matron questioned me about my activities on the island. I told her the truth.

"At least you're honest about it. That's more than I can say for other girls who are brought in," said the matron with an air of boredom.

At nine o'clock the matron took me into a small room where a judge was seated behind a desk. I saw the officer who had arrested me last night. He gave me an apologetic look as I was told to sit down. The judge asked me to state my name and address.

"You are charged with vagrancy. Do you plead guilty or not guilty?" he asked.

"I must be guilty," I confessed, though I was not sure what they meant by vagrancy.

"Does she have a record?" The judge turned to the matron.

"No, but she admitted quite candidly that she makes her living as a prostitute. She's worked for Evaline Reisner."

The judge winced. "Why in hell can't Evaline keep her girls in line?"

"She doesn't work there any longer," the matron explained.

"Well, she ought to," he said petulantly. "I don't like this business of having girls running around on the street." Suddenly he turned to me. "We try to be lenient with first offenders and because you've told the truth we'll be lenient with you. The next time you'll spend sixty days in jail. Do you understand?"

"Yes."

"And one other thing," he said before he let me go, "does it ever occur to you girls that it's a lot safer to earn a living legitimately? Why in the name of common sense can't you see that? Don't you know you'll end up a penniless old hag?"

Before I could think of any answers to his questions

97

I was shown out of the room. In the hall they told me I was free to go home.

The breakfast they had given me at six o'clock had been unsatisfactory. I stopped in a drug store three blocks away and perched myself on a stool at the counter. I ordered a sandwich and coffee.

It was nearly ten o'clock when I arrived at the apartment. Audrey was asleep on the couch, but she awoke as I prepared for a shower.

"Did you do any business last night?" she asked, raising up on one elbow.

"I spent the night in jail," I said tonelessly.

Audrey leaped up. She demanded all the particulars. When I finished, she groaned. I did not see what harm had been done, providing I behaved in the future, but Audrey straightened me out about that quick.

"I should have warned you not to solicit along Kalakaua," said the Chinese girl in deep agitation. "They're awfully touchy about that. The trouble now is that they have your name and they know you. They'll watch you and they'll watch our apartment. And I guess they'll watch me too."

"You mean we can't have any more customers?" The last person in the world I wanted to see involved in my troubles was this good, kind girl who had made herself my friend.

"We've got to be careful how we handle things," said Audrey, pacing the floor.

I sank into a chair and stared into space. It was now obvious to me that I should no longer impose myself on Audrey. I did not want to be a burden to her or anyone else. But where could I go?

"If you wish, I'll move out right now, Audrey?" I offered.

"Who said anything about that?" she snapped.

CHAPTER THIRTEEN

I tried to keep Gil out of my thoughts during the next two days, but I did pay him one visit at the hospital. It had to be short. I had remembered the offer made to me by Johnny Takoga, the photographer, and with the urgency of needed funds hanging over my head, I was determined to make money any way I could.

The change in Gil's attitude was even more pronounced during the brief visit. I sensed that his sentiments had definitely turned away from the love he had once professed. He left no doubt but that he was fond of me, but in the same manner that he was fond of Audrey. The deeper emotions were no longer apparent. Instead, he was lighthearted and gay. He had been glad to see me, but did not seem unduly distressed by my departure.

I was accustomed to facing facts and now the evidence was quite clear: Gil no longer loved me. It was what I had wanted. From the very beginning I had known that only tragedy could ensue from our love. I had deliberately discouraged him. But now that I had achieved my goal, I was left with an empty feeling and a sadness tightening about my throat. Melancholy engulfed my mind like a cloud as I went from the hospital to Johnny Takoga's photographic studio.

"Well, hello there," said Johnny Takoga, getting up from his desk when I walked in.

99

"Do you remember me?"

"I forget faces once in a while, but never figures. Especially one like yours. How's Mrs. Reisner?"

"I haven't seen her for some time. I'm no longer working for her," I said.

He motioned me to a chair. His eyes roved over me professionally. "You've got on to bigger things, I'll bet. When the Madam brought you here I thought to myself that she couldn't keep you very long. You're too good-looking to be wasting your time at her place."

I made no comment. There was no point in confessing that Mrs. Reisner had ordered me out.

"You mentioned when I was here the other time that you need models once in a while," I said.

Johnny nodded as he gave me a speculative look. "What sort of photography did you especially have in mind? I do two kinds here. One is an under the table deal. The other is for advertising illustrations."

"I'm only interested in making some extra money."

"What's your phone number?"

I told him. "The best time to reach me is mornings and early afternoons."

"Okay, baby. You'll be hearing from me."

I thanked him and left. The interview had sounded encouraging. That evening while Audrey and I were eating our dinner at the kitchen table, I reported my visit to the photographer.

"Why, you little idiot!" Audrey exclaimed, throwing down her fork.

I stared open-mouthed. I had thought Audrey would be pleased at my attempts to make extra money.

"It isn't enough that you got your name registered at the police headquarters. Now you're figuring on getting your picture plastered all over town, advertising yourself as a whore!" Audrey raged.

100

"But he pays good modeling fees. He said so," I replied.

"Do you know what for? Pictures of you in action! I know Takoga, and I know girls who have posed for him. Damn it to hell! Once he circulates pictures of you, you'll be ruined but good!"

I was at a loss as to what was expected of me. I could not understand the strange Western attitudes. A geisha's work was to entertain men. In Japan it was as simple as that. You made a living and no one complained.

But here, though a girl's profession was recognized by the clientele, it was denied at every turn. The authorities who had locked me up admitted prostitution on one hand while refusing it on the other. I understood the necessity for certain restrictions. Yet, I had difficulty understanding the fine line that was drawn between ethics within the realm of the profession itself.

"Look," said Audrey. "I think you'd better make up your mind right now whether you want to work at Waikiki or go on down to River Street."

"Isn't the only difference in working conditions?" I asked.

Audrey glanced at me quickly. She started to say something then stopped, her eyes filled with thought. Suddenly her smile was friendly.

"By golly, kid, maybe I've just begun to sense what your trouble is. Sure, there's a difference, to me. But there isn't to most people. I'm not high-hat and I know you aren't either. But you're better off here than you were at Evaline Reisner's. And you'd be better off at Evaline's than you would be on River Street."

"I made more money at Mrs. Reisner's than I have here. And certainly I had much more left over," I pointed out.

101

"Yes, but you're your own boss. That's the big difference. Americans like their independence. Doesn't that mean anything to you?"

"Yes." But I was still a bit confused.

Audrey cocked her head quizzically. "Here you can choose your own friends. At Mrs. Reisner's did you have a nice neighbor like Gil Dawson?"

The circle of my thoughts was completed. At the mention of Gil, I was suddenly confronted with my own emotions, though I hadn't the remotest notion that our relationship ever would be straightened. That was the difference, I presumed, between the Orient and the West. In Japan a geisha is respected. It was different with American men!

"Then you don't think I ought to do business with Johnny Takoga?" I sighed.

"Not unless he wants you to pose for legitimate pictures."

Fortunately I got a call that evening. It helped my morale. It was from a man I had entertained two weeks ago. If he was as generous this time as he had been on the first occasion, I would come home with good money tonight.

"Stay off the streets," Audrey suggested when I left at nine o'clock. "The police will have an eye on you."

"Not if I see them first," I laughed.

My date was with a bachelor who lived alone in a modern house high on Alencaster overlooking the city. We had some drinks as we listened to his favorite hi-fi recordings and sat before a large picture window looking out over the lights of Honolulu and the dark waters of the Pacific beyond.

I leaned back against the cushions of the large divan and gazed distantly through the window. The moon reflecting on the water made a shimmering path of gold toward my homeland. I wondered if the cherry blossoms had unfolded. I thought of the early dew on the rice fields, and of the endless, colorful procession of the multitudes along the streets of Tokyo.

"A penny for your thoughts," said the gentleman by my side.

"I was thinking of the lovely night and how dark the ocean looks from this distance," I murmured.

At the same time, I wondered how much money I would leave with tonight and whether or not Gil would come home from the hospital tomorrow.

"You're gorgeous. It's worth it just to have you sitting there to look at," he said.

I had long since ceased to wonder about the reactions of some men. If he enjoyed looking at me, I certainly had no objection. He was paying for the time. Other men would have tumbled me onto a couch almost at once. Some enjoyed flirtations that prolonged their pleasure. Still others rode roughshod over every delay in their lust.

In time, my companion tired of looking at me and demanded more substantial evidence of my visit. He sent me home in a taxi at two o'clock with a hundred dollars bulging my purse.

Audrey and I awoke at noon. We had been up but a short time when we heard movement in the next apartment. Audrey called over from the kitchen.

"Hey, Gil, is that you?"

"It sure is," he replied cheerfully. "I've been waiting for you to get up. I'd like to come over. Is Kimiko there?"

"Yes. She's here."

Gil joined us a few minutes later. He wore a pair of slacks, an aloha shirt and sandals. He had lost weight in the hospital and his skin had a pallid look. The sun would correct that in a few days. He handed me a check for nearly two hundred dollars.

103

"I didn't know until I went to the office in the hospital that you had taken care of the bills," he said. "Thanks a million but naturally I can't have you out that money."

"I didn't want you to be worried while you were so sick," I explained.

There was a peculiar expression about his eyes as he looked at me. Quickly he glanced away. He began to talk of other things. Audrey invited him to join us for a cup of coffee. As the three of us sat in the living room, Gil told us that the doctor had recommended that he take it easy for a week. He was going to rest and spend a lot of time on the beach. After that he was anxious to get on with his plans to buy the gift shop in Hilo.

Later that afternoon, a friend called Audrey and invited her to a luau tomorrow afternoon and evening.

Four days went by and I saw very little of Gil. The two or three times we were together at the apartment were brief, for he always seemed to have something to do. And always his attitude was one of neighborliness and friendship, though a couple of times I felt that it was forced.

One afternoon when I returned to the apartment after shopping, I was astounded to find Mrs. Reisner sitting in the living room talking with Audrey.

"Hello, Kimiko," she said with surprising cordiality.

"Good afternoon, Mrs. Reisner." I had not lost my respect for the woman.

She wasted no time getting to the purpose of her visit.

"I'm afraid my firing you was the result of a misunderstanding. I wish to apologize and offer you your old job back."

I sat down, wondering what this was all about. I

104

looked at Mrs. Reisner, then at Audrey. Seeing my bewilderment, Mrs. Reisner went on.

"Your neighbor, Mr. Dawson, called on me and told
me that I had been wrong to think that you were oper-
ating on your own away from my place."

I looked down. Why had Gil done that?

"Would you like to work for me again?"

When I looked up I saw Audrey out of the range of
Mrs. Reisner's vision signaling frantically with her head
to say no. I gave the Madam a grateful smile.

"Thanks kindly for the offer, Mrs. Reisner, but Audrey
and I are getting along fairly well. There are drawbacks
to the way we live, but then I come and go as I please."

"Naturally. The whole point is, are you making the
sort of money you want?" Mrs. Reisner asked.

"We manage," I said.

"Think it over, Kimiko. I'll keep the offer open a few
days. If you decide to come back, give me a call and
I'll send Joe around with the car."

When she was gone I looked at Audrey wonderingly.
"Why do you suppose Gil went to Mrs. Reisner?"

"Haven't the faintest clue. But I'm damned sure why
the woman came to see you."

"Yes?" I gave her a questioning look.

"You were popular. That's why. She's a pretty shrewd
old dame. When she has to fire a girl who's making
money for her, she feels it—right where it hurts most, in
the pocketbook."

"But I still can't figure why Gil—"

But before the night was over I understood everything. Later that afternoon Gil invited us over for cocktails. While we were drinking, Audrey ran next door to
answer the telephone. She came back to inform us that
she had to leave on a date. Gil and I were left alone.

There was nothing artificial about his gaiety as we
chatted. In time he asked if I was busy this evening.

105

When I said I wasn't, he insisted upon taking me out
to dinner. We finished our drinks, ate at a good restaurant on the Ala Wai and were back in his apartment by
ten o'clock.

He turned on the radio. It was pleasant sitting there
with him, with the lights turned low, the fragrance of
hibiscus and ginger blossoms scenting the Hawaiian
night. All at once he startled me by taking me in his
arms.

"You must never return to that house in the Nuuanu
Valley. You must never go back to your old way of life,
Kimiko," he said.

"But, Gil, I'm still—"

He shut off my words with a kiss. The pressure of his
lips sent the blood racing through my veins. For a wild
moment I held him as if I'd never let him go. Reason
surged back against my emotion. I tried to push him
away.

"There's no difference in what I'm doing now."

"Don't say that! Don't talk about it," he ordered.

All at once I realized that Gil was attempting to see
me, not as I was, but as he wanted me to be. That would
never do. Later he would not be able to forget the life
from which I had come.

"Gil, you mustn't," I begged as he kissed me again
and again.

I tried to restrain him, but his strength overpowered
me. The control that had been mine on countless occasions deserted me. My emotion was swept up into his
own desires. I had only a brief second to tell myself how
wrong this was, before I succumbed to a need that was
greater than anything I had ever known. His touch
electrified me. I was his. And, at least for this night, Gil
was mine.

CHAPTER FOURTEEN

Gil flew down to Hilo the following afternoon to negotiate for the gift shop. He was to be gone several days.

"The longer he stays away, the better off you'll be," Audrey advised succinctly.

This followed my confession about what had happened last night. I was miserable. There was no longer any doubt as to my feeling about Gil. And now I knew that, even though the love was returned, it was a love with no chance for success.

"You sure can't make any money spending the night with Gil Dawson. What are you going to do when he comes back?" said Audrey.

"I don't know."

"If he's really gone on you, he isn't going to like it if you continue to shack up with other men. Where will that leave you?"

"I don't know that either," I said dispiritedly.

"Well, you'd better make up your mind. I can't afford to carry you. Either forget him or marry him. One or the other. But whichever it is, you've got to decide quick."

Audrey got into her swim trunks. She invited me to join her for a dip in the ocean. I liked the idea. It might clear my mind and resurrect my common sense.

107

We went to the beach. After a swim I lay down on the warm sand.

I thought back over my life, of the girls I had known who had married out of the profession. There had been many, of course. I could have married, too. It would have been different in Japan where a geisha's status was different. But in the Western world few men wanted their names associated with a harlot in marriage.

Gil's proposal, if it came, would only be due to his self-imposed blindness to my past. But I knew that he could not ignore it forever.

I had to get Gil out of my mind for good. My resolve grew as I lay on the sand thinking it all out. Audrey was surfboard riding with some friends. When she came back an hour later I told her of my intentions.

"That makes sense, but will you feel that way when he's around?" Audrey asked, smiling from the corners of her eyes.

"I've got to," I said grimly.

It wasn't as easy as I had thought. Even before Gil returned five days later, I had to fight my heart. At the apartment I was diverted by Audrey's vapid chatter when she was around. But when I was alone I caught myself thinking of Gil and wishing that he were next door.

I discovered one antidote. It was the whiskey that we kept in the pantry. On two occasions, when I was alone, I downed a few drinks to help strengthen my resolve. I drank more when I was out on dates than had been my custom. And the night before Gil returned I got drunk. It might not have happened if a letter had not come from Gil saying that he had purchased the gift shop and was returning to Oahu by plane in the morning to give up the apartment. He had added a post-script that said:

"Why don't you plan to come back to Hilo with me and see how you like the place?"

"Are you going?" asked Audrey, as we dressed that evening.

"Of course not."

I leaned over a mirror to put on lipstick. I saw Audrey's reflection looking at me. There was an amused smile on her face.

"I'll be interested in seeing how you handle Gil when he gets back."

"Right now I'm more interested in a drink. How about fixing us a couple since you're already dressed?" I asked.

"You've sort of taken to the stuff, all of a sudden, haven't you?" Audrey observed.

Maybe I had, but I saw no harm in it. Audrey went to the kitchen and made two highballs. I drained mine in less than five minutes and downed a second one before we left for the party.

We had been invited that night to the home of Alonzo Smith on the Kahala Beach beyond Diamond Head. Alonzo was himself a personality around the island. He was a small dark man with considerable wealth and many friends from all over the world. His home was filled with curios that he had picked up during voyages far south to Polynesia, Melanesia and Samoa. His parties were as curious as his home. It delighted him to include among his guests a few girls who would make the occasion memorable to his visitors from the mainland.

Tonight he was entertaining a banker from Chicago and a lawyer from New York. When Audrey and I arrived, the party already was under way. Several friends who were residents of the island had been invited, but for them the party would end around midnight. Audrey and I would stay on, for however long our services were required.

"You sure know some good-looking people, Alonzo," the banker exclaimed when he was introduced to us.

"Everyone is good-looking out here, especially after a few drinks. Come on, girls, and meet the other guests," cried Alonzo merrily.

I met Victor Morgan, the lawyer from New York, a dark, handsome man whose eyes lighted up with interest as he looked at me. He immediately took my arm and led me to the bar which occupied one corner of Alonzo's living room.

"What are you, Kimiko, a Japanese girl?"

"Yes."

"But born here in Hawaii, is that it?"

"No, until not long ago I lived in Tokyo. That is my home."

Victor seemed enchanted. He asked questions as we stood at the bar drinking vodka. I told him about my life, omitting only the method by which I earned a living. This was Victor's first visit to the islands. It was his first trip beyond the continental limits of the United States. He kept me supplied with drinks.

By nine-thirty the guests numbered fourteen. Alonzo showed some motion pictures which he had filmed on his trip to the South Seas. Sandwiches and coffee were served at eleven-thirty and by midnight many guests were departing.

I had lost track of the amount of liquor I had drunk. I laughed and flirted with the men who surrounded me and accepted more drinks, all too willingly. The climax of my evening came at about twelve-thirty. I was back at the bar with Victor. We were the only ones in the room. Everything was calm. My mind seemed unusually clear. Victor tilted my face up with his hands and kissed me.

"I'd give anything for a girl such as you," he said quietly.

"Very well."

"What?" He glanced at me puzzled. Alonzo had not told his guests about Audrey and me, or why he had hired us to come. He preferred to let the men find out for themselves.

"You can have me if you wish," I said.

Victor's jaw dropped. He glanced fearfully over his shoulder to see if anyone had heard. We were alone. Audrey and the banker had gone out on the lanai overlooking the ocean. Alonzo was off somewhere in another part of the house. He bent closer to me.

"Did I hear correctly?" he asked.

I did not know what he was concerned about. "I said you could have me if you wish."

Victor reached for a bottle of Scotch. He poured himself a stout drink. I had one with him. As we stood together, he studied me for a moment then put his hands on my waist. I smiled at him. His hands moved over my hips.

"Maybe I'm only dreaming this. If I am I'll get a rude awakening, but I've got to see if this is really true," he announced.

He took me in his arms. His hands explored my body boldly as he kissed me. I pressed against him. He said he was not dreaming. Victor poured us some more drinks. I downed them willingly. I was in no hurry. I had all night. Victor didn't want to offend his host by any disorderly conduct in his home.

"I don't think he'll mind at all if we retire to one of the bedrooms," I suggested. As I spoke I realized that my speech was growing thick from drink.

"Let's go, sweetheart," he said.

An attack of dizziness struck me as I lay with Victor in another room. It was not from his passion. Indeed,

111

I was hardly aware of it. My insides were suddenly on fire and I wanted to be rid of him, without knowing why.

When he fell asleep at my side I arose. The room tilted as I stood by the bed. The furniture was blurred to my vision. Suddenly the room righted itself and I began to dress. My mind was numb. I didn't know what I was doing. In a state of partial nudity, I staggered out of the room.

"I'm seeing things," exclaimed the banker who was standing at the bar fondling Audrey.

I came across the living room. The banker stared, his eyes bulging and a broad smile on his face. He had drunk his share tonight. Audrey was feeling good, but she was sober enough to realize that I was quite drunk. Suddenly the banker turned to Audrey.

"Why don't you undress like that?" he suggested.

"You haven't asked me to," the Chinese girl teased.

"I'm asking you right now."

"Okay, but first let's take care of Kimiko. What do you want, kid? More drinks for you and Vic?"

"Yes," I muttered. "But you and your frien' go on. I can fix Vic up."

"Are you sure?" Audrey regarded me carefully.

"Sure I'm sure." I waved my arm. "Go on. Get undressed. You heard what the man said."

Audrey smiled. Just before she left with the banker she lowered her voice and spoke to me. "Take it easy, kid. I wouldn't drink any more if I were you."

She wasn't me and at that point I didn't care about anything. Suddenly I was alone in the room. Nothing made sense except the bar in front of me. I poured myself a drink and hung my elbow on the bar. I swayed as I drained the glass. I picked up the bottle to take to Victor, though why he would want it when he was asleep I did not know. I was confused and my mind would not function.

Directions meant nothing. Instead of finding myself back in the bedroom, I was in a starlit garden. There was something wrong about that. I took another drink, hoping it would clear my head. I stumbled and fell. For a while I lay on cool grass. It could have been a few minutes or hours for all I knew.

Later I was aware of pavement under my feet as I moved again, trying to find my way back into the house. Suddenly headlights glared in my eyes and I heard the screeching of tires. It came to me as if from a great distance. Only fragmentary thoughts connected my mind and awareness to what was happening. People stood about me, talking excitedly. I wanted to ask what was going on when a distant siren came to my ears. The next thing I knew, two policemen were asking me who I was and where I came from.

"Tokyo," I told them, getting the words out with considerable difficulty.

"She's nuts. We'd better take her in," said one of the cops.

A vague alarm sounded in my mind. The police. The matron. The cell. And the judge. Those thoughts flashed across my mind and I trembled like a coward. I couldn't have that. The judge would make me leave the islands. I began to weep hysterically.

Suddenly Alonzo appeared on Kahala Avenue. He had heard the commotion and came out to see what it was about. His garden fronted on the street and it was through that exit that I had wandered. A few discreet words to the police and they drove away as Alonzo led me back into the house.

I collapsed on a divan and was aware of nothing until a bright morning sun blazed into my aching eyes. Someone had covered me with a beach robe. I was so miserable that I couldn't move. How long I had lain there, or what time it was I hadn't the faintest recollection. Audrey came in from the kitchen and spoke when she found that I was awake.

"That was quite a binge you were on last night, my friend," she said mirthlessly.

"I'm still on it. I feel awful."

"Ordinarily I wouldn't suggest it, but I think a hair of the dog that bit you might be in order."

Audrey went to the bar and came back with a jigger of whiskey. I shuddered.

"Get that out of my sight," I groaned.

"Drink it," Audrey ordered, "or I'll force it down you. We've got to get out of here, and you aren't even dressed yet."

I did as I was told. The liquor burned all the way down. I felt as if I had swallowed a bad dose of medicine. For a frightening moment I thought I was going to be sick. The drink held and I sat up groggily. Audrey came back with my clothes.

With her help I was able to get dressed. The liquor I had drunk gave me strength but it was already working on my mind. Audrey called a taxi and, in a few minutes, we were on our way home.

"What in hell happened to you last night?" Audrey asked.

"Everything," I said lamely.

"Alonzo told me he found you out on the street nearly naked with a couple of coppers about to haul you into the station."

I shuddered, for I did not remember it clearly.

"Know what would happen to you?" asked Audrey. "Right now you'd be sitting in jail for keeps. Either that or you'd be on your way out of Hawaii. Don't forget, the police have your number. You've got to keep away from them."

114

I thought that over gloomily. It might be just as well if I did leave the islands. Nothing was working out right. I had hoped to find peace and security. Instead, I had run into the most hopeless involvement of my life. If I left, I might be able to forget Gil. He would forget me. Of that I was sure!

"I'm sorry I ruined the party last night," I said apologetically. "I don't suppose Alonzo will want to hire me again after causing him so much trouble."

"Don't worry about that. You went over big with the lawyer and I think I managed to give the banker some memories of Hawaii. No, Alonzo has no complaint. He was more concerned about you and the police."

"Were they going to arrest him, too?" I asked.

"No, but he had to do some fast talking to keep you out of trouble."

Alonzo's fast talk hadn't satisfied the police. When we arrived home, a man, who had been sitting in a car at the curb, followed us to the apartment. He showed a badge and said he wished to have a talk with me. I waited apprehensively as he came in and glanced around the apartment.

"We have a report on you at headquarters. You were running around in your birthday suit out on Kahala Avenue last night," said the man.

"She was drunk, officer," Audrey spoke up.

"Makes no difference. She was working Kalakaua not too long ago. Now this! You girls get by pretty easy, everything considered, but when you get so damned brazen as to run around naked in respectable neighborhoods that's when we draw the line," he replied firmly.

"She wasn't working out there last night. I told you she was drunk. We were at a party."

"What kind of a party was it where a girl trots around without her clothes?" he asked cynically.

"It was a private party," Audrey answered.

115

"Look, we don't care what happens inside a man's house, so long as it doesn't disturb anyone. But we can't have girls out on the street stopping traffic."

"I'm guilty. There's no doubt of that," I said dejectedly. "Do you want me to go to the police station now?"

"I didn't say that," the man snapped. "I didn't come here to arrest you. That should have happened last night, but it didn't. I'm here to give you a final warning. If we have any more trouble with you, you're through on this island. Understand?"

I nodded wearily. At least I wasn't being arrested again. That was a break. I was worn out and discouraged. Nothing mattered much.

The detective gave the apartment another brief scrutiny as if he expected to find evidence of vice in that small room. He glanced at both of us sternly, then turned and walked out. Audrey and I looked at each other in silence.

"They'll be riding you pretty hard for a while. You'll have to lay low until it blows over," said Audrey finally.

I lit a cigarette. My hand was shaking. I sat down to relieve my legs which suddenly felt as if they could not support me. Though I felt wretched with shame for what I had done, a seed of resentment was taking root inside me. It was not the healthy kind. It was ugly and bitter. At the moment I wanted to destroy myself.

"I'll go to River Street and work. That's where I belong, anyway."

CHAPTER FIFTEEN

"Don't be a fool. River Street is for dames who can't do any better," said Audrey.

"I can't see where I'm doing so well." I gave a hollow laugh.

"What are you worried about? You've got some money. You can get by for a couple of weeks or longer if you have to."

"It's no good for you, me being around here. They'll watch you too."

"I can take care of myself," Audrey replied. "You're the one who's hot. And if you behave yourself for a while they'll let up on you. I don't mind you being here, so long as you pay half."

Audrey Ching was one of the few unselfish people in my life. I could not understand her feeling of friendship toward me. My contribution had been nothing but trouble for her. Yet, here she was, still trying to help me, still offering to share her way of life. I thanked her with my eyes.

"What I ought to do is go back to Tokyo," I said.

"And get a knife in your back? Isn't that what you said they tried to do to you?"

"Maybe they've lost interest in me by now."

"You wouldn't catch me taking that sort of chance!" Audrey said emphatically. "You'd be crazy to go back. Anyway, what's there in Tokyo?"

"I would be home, among people who understand my occupation. There is so much the other world does not know or comprehend about a geisha." I gave a little gesture intended to include all of Hawaii with its American ways.

"Look, Kimiko," said Audrey, and her voice was tolerant and kind. "You've had a lot of tough luck, and you've had some bad breaks in Hawaii. But things will pick up. You're going through an adjustment. That's all. Don't let it get you down. Right now you're nervous and upset. Why don't you have another bracer to calm your nerves, then we'll both grab some sleep. You'll feel much better after that."

Without waiting for a reply Audrey went to the pantry and came back with a bottle and two glasses. She poured a drink for me and one for herself. She downed hers quickly, then got out of her clothes and stretched comfortably on the couch.

"Oh brother, am I tired! That banker was no angel. How was your guy?"

"I don't remember," I said truthfully.

I drained my glass and took off my dress. Audrey was already asleep. Before I joined her I had another drink. I wanted to anesthetize my mind against any thought at all. Nothing had bothered me last night except a physical discomfort. If I drank enough, but not too much, maybe I could achieve a state of suspended animation in which I could live without hurt, physical or mental. As I was about to lie down I glanced through the screen and saw Gil crossing the court.

A pang stabbed my heart as I watched him go on to his own apartment and heard him moving about inside. Before I joined Audrey, I swallowed again from the bottle. As I lay down and closed my eyes, Gil called through the back door.

"Anybody awake in there?"

118

I bit my lip to keep from answering. In a final, clear flash of reason I knew that I didn't dare get up and let Gil in while I was drunk. He called a second time but even as his words died away, I drifted off into an alcoholic slumber.

The process of awakening, that afternoon, was slow and painful. My mouth was dry. The muscles of my thighs ached. Though my skin was dry, I felt hot and tense inside. For a long time I lay with my eyes shut, hoping that sleep would come again, but knowing that it wouldn't. At last I sat up. Audrey was gone, perhaps to the beach for a swim. I went to the bathroom and drank two glasses of cold water. I turned on the shower and stepped under it, letting the cold water revive me.

Fifteen minutes under the shower gave me a new start on life. I felt better but my nerves were still on edge. I couldn't understand the tension that gripped me like an electric current. What was wrong? I had a little money. Loafing around the apartment for a week or so wouldn't be strenuous. The police would be off my neck by then and I could go back to work. My thoughts strung themselves along with soundest logic. Still, something was wrong. I knew it instinctively.

Audrey came in from the beach at five o'clock. As she was rolling her swim trunks down from her hips, she mentioned that she had talked with Gil earlier that afternoon. I was instantly attentive.

"He said to ask you to wait here for him. He went to Honolulu on business and will be back around five-thirty or six," said Audrey.

"I'm not going anywhere," I remarked. "What does he want with me?"

"He wants to tell you about the deal he made in Hilo."

"He bought the gift shop?"

"Yes."

That meant that Gil would be moving away soon.

Probably in the next day or two. He couldn't run a business in Hilo and still live at Waikiki. His absence might be the very thing I needed to overcome my nervousness. Much of my uncertainty was due to my conflicting thoughts about Gil. With this new hope, I already felt a light relief from my agitation.

While Audrey dressed for her dinner date, I made some drinks. Audrey was surprised and remarked that she'd never seen me drink so much.

In moments of complete sobriety I knew this to be true myself. Liquor had always been something to guard against in my homeland. A geisha was disgraced if she drank too much. Yet, here it seemed like the thing to do. People actually expected it of girls such as myself. I was torn with doubt, yet I had found some uses for alcohol.

Gil arrived at six o'clock just as Audrey was leaving. He eyed us both gleefully.

"Everything is set," he announced. "I'm moving over to the big island tomorrow."

"I wish I could stick around to help give you a going-away party tonight. But I'll have to leave that up to Kimiko," said Audrey. "Will I see you in the morning before you leave?"

"Sure thing." He grinned as Audrey went out.

He turned to me and took me in his arms. I tried to control the pounding of my heart. He smiled down at me. He kissed me, then asked, "Want to hear about it?"

"You know I do, Gil."

He spent the next half-hour telling me about the little shop he had bought. It would never make him rich but it would provide a good income after he had built it up some. His eagerness was contagious and I found myself enthused with thoughts of the shop.

"But I don't want to bore you with all of this on an

empty stomach. Let's go to dinner. We can talk there," he said.

I agreed but as we were leaving I said as an afterthought, "Could we go some place different, Gil? I'd like to get away from Waikiki."

I did not explain that my purpose was to avoid being seen by the police. Gil was happy to oblige. We drove around to the other side of the island to a restaurant overlooking Kaneohe Bay. There, at a table for two, we enjoyed a good dinner as the moon came up over the eastern rim of the Pacific.

"I have other plans beside the gift shop, Kimiko," he said, gazing at me tenderly as we sat over our coffee.

I searched his eyes and what I saw in them made me look away quickly.

"You probably already know what I mean. Don't you?" he smiled.

"No. I—I don't think so." I dreaded to hear it; though not to hear it would have plunged me into an even greater unhappiness for the rest of my life.

"It's about you and me." He paused. "I want to marry you," he said, his voice suddenly husky.

My mind was in a maelstrom of contradictions. How happy we could be! But how tragic would be the end, when it came. I felt my face contorted with anguish.

"You—you don't know what you're saying, Gil. You haven't thought it out at all."

"But I have, sweetheart. I want you. Nothing else matters."

"It will, later on. You'll remember things about me. Things you'll think of more and more and that never can be erased," I said bitterly.

"I was in love with another girl, once. Would you think of that?"

"No, Gil. Not in a thousand years," I groaned.

121

"Then why should I think of your—" he hesitated and a peculiar look crossed his eyes.

That was enough for me to know that I was right. When the honeymoon was over, he'd remember. He would, no matter how desperately he tried not to. I shook my head wearily.

"You will. You're human," I said.

"All right then, so what? Why should that keep us from happiness?"

"Because the happiness you think of now is only an illusion, Gil. We would be wonderfully happy. Then one day it would be over and, try as you may, you could never look at me again as you have."

"But if I promised—"

"I should never expect you to keep it. No man could do the impossible. No man could entirely forget."

"Don't say that!" he said irritably. "If I'm willing to forget, you should be also!"

"Willing, yes!" I said, my eyes heavy with sadness, "but I'm only human too. I would think of it when I saw accusation in your eyes."

"You'll never see it," he pleaded.

I gazed at him. He wanted me now. No matter what; but I knew that a lasting marriage in the Western world could never be built on the foundation of my life. Men in the grip of passion had vowed everlasting love and had scorned even to acknowledge me on the street the next morning. It would be that way with Gil some day. His mind could never forget what I once had been.

"I'm sorry, Gil," I said in almost a whisper. "For your sake, it just can't ever be."

"You're not even willing to give me a chance. That's not fair," he complained.

"It's the only way."

Gil shook his head. "I'm going to make you think differently."

He paid the check and we left the restaurant. We drove back along the Kalanianaole road, stopping at Makapuu Point to watch some torch fishermen. Far out-in the Kaiwi Channel were the winking lights of a ship bound for a mainland port. It was midnight when we reached home. Gil insisted that I come to his apartment.

"This is where you begin to change your mind," he smiled as he embraced me.

For a second I had an impulse to resist. But there could be no clean break between us. I could not deny him this last night. Having submitted to the passions of countless men, it was absurd that I should hesitate with the one man I loved. His mouth came down on mine.

I was drawn to him at once, wanting him as much as he wanted me. It frightened me. I steeled myself against being persuaded to change my mind. For, in the weakness of my love, it was entirely possible that emotion would overcome logic. Gil's hands were firm and demanding.

I tried desperately to make my mind and body react only as they would with others. But the throbbing of my heart and the yearning that vibrated through every nerve in my body quickly swept away my attempt at pretense. With a whimper I gave up and let emotion lead me.

"You're mine. You've got to be for always, from now on," he said.

In the roar of the rapture that followed, I wanted nothing more than to believe what he said. I gave myself to him with abandon, caring only for the great passion we shared. And if, at that moment he had insisted, I would have promised to go with him to the ends

123

of the earth. But in the quiet contentment that followed, I knew this had to be the end.

"You do love me. Let me hear you say it," Gil murmured.

"Yes, Gil. I love you."

"You're going to Hilo with me. We'll be married over
there."

I did not answer.

"Say that you will," he insisted.

"I can't, Gil."

"I won't let you go until you promise," he warned.

"I can't make a promise that couldn't be kept."

I lifted my arms and entwined them around his neck.
Our lips met. Our bodies were in agreement, if our
thoughts were not.

CHAPTER SIXTEEN

Though my heart was heavy over Gil's imminent departure, I managed to appear gay the next morning. He was busy until noon packing his things and arranging for their shipment along with his car to the big island. I made sandwiches for our lunch and as we ate he again tried to talk me into going with him.

"Let's not argue, Gil. In a while you'll be gone. Let's remember our last day together with happiness as we will remember our last night," I begged.

"What makes you think this is so final?" he asked.

"It has to be," I said pensively.

"That's what you think. I'll be back in a week or so. And I'll keep coming back until you agree to marry me," he announced flatly.

I gave him a tragic look. "No, Gil, you mustn't!"

He smiled, but said no more. All at once I knew that nothing had been settled. He would come back. I would see him again, even though I tried to avoid it. I didn't know what to do.

Then, suddenly, it was time for him to go. He phoned for a taxi and while we waited he held me in his arms. My heart broke and I was unable to check my tears. Before I knew it the taxi was outside.

"See you next week," he said and kissed me good-bye.

I was so choked up that I could say nothing. Through the mist that covered my eyes I watched him get in the taxi. He waved. The taxi pulled away from the curb and headed for the airport.

I was asleep on the couch when Audrey came home later that afternoon. Her movement awakened me and I sat up. My face was white and I felt empty, drained of all emotion. Audrey, frightened by my pallor, asked if I felt all right.

"Yes," I replied listlessly.

"Did you get Gil off?"

"Yes, but he said he'd be back next week. He still thinks I might marry him."

"You'd both be a damned sight better off if you did," Audrey chuckled.

My mind ached from thinking about it. I said no more.

The next two days moved by with tedious monotony. The evenings were long and dull with Audrey out. I sat alone in the apartment, reading, listening to the radio and drinking whenever I caught myself thinking of Gil. My nerves began to tighten.

It wouldn't have been so bad if I could have left the apartment, but Audrey insisted that the police weren't fooling. I had to be careful for a week at least.

"Would I get in trouble if I went out to Mrs. Reisner's Friday and Saturday?" I asked.

"Go ahead, if that's how you feel. But why just for the week-end?" asked Audrey, glancing at me sharply.

"That's when they're the busiest. Mrs. Reisner might let me work those two nights."

"This looks like the end of a beautiful friendship. I thought we could make a go of it but it doesn't look that way now," said Audrey laconically.

"I don't intend to go back there permanently."

"Reisner won't have it any other way."

"If she says no, then I won't go," I said.

That evening when Audrey was gone I called the

Madam. Mrs. Reisner needed a girl and could use me very handily but she balked at letting me work two nights only. I was about to give up when Mrs. Reisner, unwilling to lose a chance at getting me back, told me she'd send Joe in the car to pick me up tomorrow afternoon.

I took with me only enough clothes for the week-end. I hoped to reassure Audrey that I was not leaving permanently by refusing to take all of my things. I arrived at the house in time for dinner the following evening. Betty and Colette said they were glad to see me, but they were not overly enthusiastic. Vanessa was gone. Two other girls whom I had not met before were there.

Friday night went fine, but Saturday was off to a bad start when one of my customers wanted to do some drinking. Forgetting my old habit of being able to sip my liquor without ever taking very much, I went right along with him.

Later in the evening several guests complained to Mrs. Reisner that I was tipsy.

"That will be all for you, Kimiko!" said Mrs. Reisner storming in. "You know that I don't tolerate drunks. Get out of here!"

I knew a moment of guilt but I had reached the point where I didn't really care. I was tired. I didn't want any more customers tonight anyway. I apologized to Mrs. Reisner but the woman only glared. Slowly I got into my clothes.

Joe let me out at the apartment an hour later. Audrey was gone. Wearily I got ready for bed. I poured myself a nightcap and downed it. I stretched out, glad to be back at a place I could call home. Though Gil no longer lived next door, it was nice to think of him being associated with this place. I fell into a deep sleep.

"Imagine my surprise, finding you here when I got in

early this morning," Audrey told me the next day. "Did something happen out at Reisner's?"

"Yes. I drank too much with one of the customers."

Audrey laughed. "It serves her right! I'm glad you're through there. But your drinking is something else. I've noticed you've let yourself go pretty much. You've got to behave or you'll get in serious trouble."

"I know."

"You surely haven't gotten so you like the stuff." The Chinese girl regarded me shrewdly.

"No, but a little drink once in a while doesn't hurt."

"The hell it doesn't. You'd better lay off for a while. I've noticed several signs about your drinking—none of them good, kid. Take it from a friend, you're hitting the bottle too heavy," Audrey said crisply.

I knew that was true. I had discovered it long before Audrey. The point was, I didn't care. A drink was no solution to my problem of Gil. All I wanted was temporary relief from my aching unhappiness. I was fleeing from myself, and knew it.

Gil was back in Honolulu the following week. He attended to some business during the day and spent the evening with me at the apartment. Being with him was sweet agony for I couldn't resist his love, nor could I give in to it the way he wanted. Our time together merely repeated the same old arguments. And when he departed for Hilo the next day I went through the same torment I had known the first time.

Alone again I moved about the apartment restlessly. Even my drinking wasn't helping me too much any more. I had to find something to occupy my time. Audrey said she thought the police would let me alone and that by the week-end I might be able to entertain once more. But the week-end was still three days off. I had to do something. I had only the life I had known to cling to. In

128

desperation I went into Honolulu one afternoon and called on Johnny Takoga.

"You want to make some pictures with me?" he smiled as he welcomed me into his studio.

"No. I wonder if you could put me in touch with one of the houses besides Mrs. Reisner's. I need work," I told him.

"I sure can. The Sandman runs a pretty lively place and he's a friend of mine," he grinned.

"Could I see him this afternoon?"

Johnny went to the telephone. He talked for several minutes. When he hung up he wrote an address on a small slip of paper and handed it to me.

"He'll see you in an hour. Be at that address," said Johnny.

I arrived at the address which was in sight of Honolulu Harbor. From the outside it looked like a store. As I mounted the stairs, I wondered if I had come to the right place. A small, grinning man met me as I reached the second floor. He introduced himself as Jack.

"You've heard of me as the Sandman," he said. He was a Eurasian. "Come with me, sweetheart."

He led me into a room that contained nothing more than a table and three ancient chairs. When he closed the door, he looked me over shrewdly.

"A pretty girl such as you can find lots of love here," he remarked.

"All I want is work," I said, looking at him evenly.

"You've worked before?"

"I was a geisha in Japan. I've worked at Mrs. Reisner's."

All at once he spoke to me in Japanese. He had lived in Osaka for several years. Strangely enough, I felt as much at ease with him as I had with anyone since leaving my homeland. He was an evil man by all standards,

129

but his evil was something I understood. In turn he showed a respect for me which he seldom had for the girls who came to him.

"You can begin work tonight if you wish," he told me.

"That's good. I wish to do that," I replied, still speaking Japanese. "I have only one reservation."

He studied me narrowly and waited for me to go on.

"If I find the work not to my liking, I shall not remain long."

"Perhaps after a night or two I can offer added inducements," he smiled slyly. I think that he hoped adding a real geisha to his establishment would increase the quality of his trade.

"I'm interested in money but right now I am equally interested in keeping myself occupied."

"You have come to the right place," said the Sandman.

I was shown to a small room with a single cot and a wash basin. There was nothing fancy about it. It was geared to a production line type of operation. There were eight such rooms in the establishment and the hall outside was heavily trafficked from eight o'clock at night until nearly dawn.

The clients were tough, lustful men for the most part whose breath smelled of cheap liquor and whose passions were hardy but quickly spent. They came from the factories, the docks and the ships. They spoke a variety of tongues and were of all nationalities.

I had no time to think of Gil, or of drinking that night. And when the last visitor lifted his rough hands from my bare shoulders and lunged out, I was so tired that I fell immediately into a deep and undisturbed slumber.

Late in the afternoon when I awoke, I had time to consider my situation. There was no happiness for me here, but there was no time for unhappiness. Perhaps this was my salvation. It was all I knew, and all I was good for. There was no place for the geisha in the Occidental world. There was only a place for her body. Already the place was beginning to stir, making ready for another night of activity.

After the second night I arose in the middle of the afternoon and told the Sandman that I needed to go home for a change of clothes.

"You'll be back, of course," he said, regarding me closely.

"Yes."

"I'm depending on that." There was a mild warning in his tone.

Audrey had just returned from the beach when I arrived at the apartment.

"Where in the hell have you been?" she demanded. "I was about to turn in an alarm for you," said the Chinese girl.

I told her. Audrey stared at me. Then suddenly she burst into a tirade.

"You little fool! You crazy mixed-up idiot! I warned you not to get involved with that crowd."

"There's no harm. That's my place. I know it now. I'm going back tonight. I can make fair money there."

"Well, just get ready to change your plans. I won't let you ruin yourself that way. Besides, there's work for you here. Plenty. Remember Walton Creet? You were with him that night we went to George's on the Windward side. He's back out here from the mainland and wants to engage your services indefinitely. I looked everywhere for you last night and—"

"Wouldn't I be running a risk with the police?" I asked.

"You're running a risk at the Sandman's. You don't know how much. I'll be surprised if we don't have trouble with him."

"This Walton Creet. What does he want of me? You say indefinitely."

"Yes and he's got money to pay for it. George says he's plenty rich. Now, just get any ideas out of your head about going back to the Sandman's. You're going to see Walton tonight."

I sat down, my face a mask of despair. Would I ever know what I was supposed to be doing in this world? Nothing was lasting. Nothing was permanent. My life in Hawaii had been a pattern of violent contrasts with the burden of a hopeless love thrown in for good measure.

"I ought to let the Sandman know," I muttered.

Audrey faced me belligerently. "If you call that cheap rat, you can get out of this apartment right now and never come back. I'm plenty sore at you for going there already."

"But—"

"You heard what I said!" Audrey's eyes flashed.

"All right, Audrey. I'll do it your way," I said tiredly.

Walton Creet had taken an apartment at Waikiki, though he was going to be in the islands less than a week. His place was only a few blocks from where Audrey and I lived. I arrived there at nine o'clock that night. The apartment was many times larger than the efficiency Audrey and I lived in. Walton was waiting for me in the living room.

"Kimiko!" He greeted me cordially when I came in. "It's so good to see you."

I had almost forgotten what he looked like. Tall and slender, he was immaculate in slacks and sport coat. He welcomed me with a kiss.

"I didn't ever expect to see you again," I told him.

"You're going to see a lot of me. Didn't your roommate explain?"

"She said you wanted my time for a few days. I wasn't

132

home last night and didn't learn of it until this afternoon."

"I know and I've been frantic to be with you. Last night I was afraid I might have made the trip for nothing. I came out especially to see you," he smiled.

I gave him a disillusioned smile. I didn't believe that for an instant. But it was true, I discovered later.

Walton served some drinks as we sat chatting for a while. He said he had been thinking about me all the time he had been gone. He wanted me to give serious consideration to returning to the mainland with him. That was nonsense to me, but I humored him. He described his home in Beverly Hills and said I would have nothing to worry about except looking pretty for him.

Later, when he held me locked in his arms, I wondered what he would think if he knew the Sandman's tawdry cubicle where I had been the night before. I sighed. Once again it was feast or famine. A night in a waterfront brothel followed by an exclusive apartment at Waikiki. What would it be next week?

As Walton and I were dining on a terrace overlooking Diamond Head two evenings later, he again mentioned the subject of my going to the United States. He wanted my decision soon for he had to make some arrangements.

"But I thought you were kidding," I said.

"Not at all. I want you to go with me," he said, in all seriousness.

When I realized what he meant, I frowned. "Under what terms, Walton? After all, I have myself to think about."

"You're my little geisha girl out here. You would be the same back there," he smiled.

"And when you tire of me?" I looked at him quite frankly.

"Who said I would?"

"I've been in this work too long to believe otherwise."

"I'll take care of you, baby. Don't worry about that." His voice was suddenly soft and caressing. "Will you go?"

"I don't know. It's an entirely new idea. I'll have to think it over, Walton."

"When can you let me know?"

"How long do I have?"

"A few days. But I must know definitely."

At first the idea had seemed a logical solution. It would take me away from the island and out of Gil's life for good. But the more I thought of it that evening and the next morning when I awoke, the more disadvantages it appeared to have. At best it was only a temporary security. The United States was a foreign land. When Walton cast me aside, what would I do? In Hawaii were some who could at least speak my language, and I wasn't thinking of Japanese. I was thinking of the language of girls such as Audrey and myself.

I was addressed in that language by the Sandman when I went to the apartment to see Audrey that afternoon. He was waiting for me when I arrived. Audrey was there too, her face dark. The Sandman bowed obsequiously when I walked in. He grinned.

"You're coming back to work for me, sweetheart," he said. "You have a choice between that or going to jail."

CHAPTER SEVENTEEN

At first I failed to catch the significance of his words. I stared at him, my eyes puzzled and brows knitted. Audrey's mouth was grim. She spoke between her teeth.

"I told you this scum would get you into trouble," she said, glancing at me, then at the Sandman.

"But I haven't done anything," I replied.

"When you failed to report to work the other night I was perturbed. Some customers have been asking for you," said the Sandman blandly. "I got to thinking that a valuable property such as you must not be permitted to waste her talents elsewhere. I have spent the past few days finding out about you, Kimiko. And I've learned some things that the Honolulu police would find rather interesting."

"They know about me. You can't tell them anything new."

"A girl who has worked at my place isn't welcome at the beach. You no longer have any place to go, sweetheart, except to return to me. If you don't, I tell the police and you go to jail. It's as simple as that. Do you see?"

"We have friends!" Audrey shouted at him.

"It would be interesting to discover if you have as many friends among the police as I do. If you're willing to make the test, so am I," he replied smoothly.

Audrey stormed about the apartment in frustration. I

sank into a chair. I was incapable of thinking straight any longer. No matter what I did it caused trouble. There was a curse on me. The Sandman looked at me smugly.

"Perhaps you cannot wind up your affairs here in a few hours. I'm a reasonable man. More customers will ask for you tonight. I must be able to tell them that you are still indisposed, but that you definitely will be available to them tomorrow night. So you have twenty-four hours to reach your decision."

He stood up. Audrey favored him with a few choice invectives which caused him to chuckle. With a friendly wave of his hand to both of us he went out.

"You see what I meant when I told you what a fool you had been? That's what he's noted for. He gets a girl in a crack then makes her knuckle under. Half the pots that work for him can't quit because he's got something on them," Audrey raged.

"I'm not going back there," I said slowly, as my mind turned to Walton's offer.

"You won't if we can find a way out. We're not licked yet. I think I'll get Alonzo to give us a hand. He's got connections."

"That won't be necessary. Walton Creet wants me to go to the United States with him. I hadn't cared about it, but now it looks like my only salvation."

Audrey gazed at me for a moment. A broad grin crossed her face. "Why didn't you tell me?"

"Because I wanted to stay here."

"A guy like Walton wants to put you up in style, yet you would rather stay here? I don't get it, Kimiko," said Audrey flatly.

I only vaguely understood it myself. But in the inner recesses of my mind I knew. I was clinging to the only spot in the world where I had known true love. Waikiki, the seawall, the beach and the apartment were enshrined in my thoughts with my love for Gil Dawson.

"When would you be leaving with him?" asked Audrey.

"I don't know."

"If he wants you badly enough you'd better make him take you away before tomorrow night. The Sandmen might be bluffing about going to the police. But you can't take a chance. You're too far out on a limb."

That night I gave Walton my answer. He was delighted. When I stipulated that I wanted to leave no later than tomorrow night, he wasn't even curious about my reason. He went to the phone and ordered two reservations on the plane that would leave the Honolulu airport for Oakland, California, tomorrow evening. He put in an overseas call and talked with someone in Beverly Hills, advising him of the time of his return.

Walton, I observed, did things in a big way. I spent the night in his apartment, then obtained his permission to leave early the next morning so I could pack my things.

He had given me three hundred dollars with which to buy luggage and a suit to wear on the plane. I knew nothing about suits that would be appropriate for such an occasion. I went to Sadie's and stated my problem. The enterprising dressmaker had just the thing— a dark, blue, lightweight gabardine with white collar and cuffs. It needed alteration but would be ready and delivered to my address at three o'clock that afternoon. At a shop on Kalakaua, I bought two pieces of luggage. I took them to the apartment in a taxi.

"Until this very moment I wondered if you were really going," said Audrey, eyeing the luggage.

"Do I have any choice?"

"Very little. But, do you know, I'm going to miss you,

Kimiko. As a roommate you've been first-rate, even though you couldn't stay out of trouble," she smiled.

"It won't be any different where I'm going. Trouble will follow me there," I said woefully.

"That's not the right attitude. But if you don't like it in America come back here. By then the Sandman and the police both will have forgotten about you."

We were both excited as I packed for the trip. Audrey never had been to the mainland but she had heard a lot more about it than I. She told me what she knew about clothes worn in Los Angeles and assured me that Walton would supply me with everything I needed. We took time out for lunch at one o'clock and were having coffee when Gil came in.

"Howdy," he cried happily. "I had to fly up this morning and have to catch the afternoon plane back, but I couldn't land on Oahu without dropping around to say hello." His eyes fell on the luggage that was opened out on the couch. "Hey, what's this? Who's going away?"

I swallowed hard. I hadn't counted on being confronted by Gil.

"I—I'm leaving, Gil," I said.

"Where are you going?" The smile vanished from his face.

"To Los Angeles."

"But, Kimiko, you can't—"

"I've got to. It's business."

"What kind of business?" He eyed me suspiciously.

I didn't know what to say. I was dismayed at seeing him. My resolve to leave him already was weakened by his presence. Audrey spoke up during the silence that threatened to engulf us.

"She's going to have a shot at the movies, Gil. No fooling. But she'll probably be back when they discover that she's no actress," Audrey laughed.

138

"I don't believe that. Why are you going?" Gil turned to me.

"I can't stay here," I said, miserable.

"You don't love me. You wouldn't be going away if you did. Are you going to marry someone?" he asked.

"Oh, no," I said quickly.

"Kimiko, you can't do this to me," he cried, grabbing hold of me. His voice was frantic. "I've been working my head off over in Hilo. And it's been all for you. I've already looked at a little home we could buy. You can't go! You can't!"

I was numb with grief. My heart pounded with indecision. If Gil didn't go soon it might wreck my plans to go away. Anything could happen after that. I would be in the hands of the Sandman, or the police. Gil and I could never remain together in any event.

"Gil, believe me," I cried. "I love you and always will. But I can't stay in Hawaii. You've got to believe me."

"She's right, Gil," said Audrey, her voice heavy with meaning.

"Will one of you explain why she can't?" Gil asked, beside himself.

"I'll tell you when she's gone. Come to the apartment the next time you're on Oahu," said Audrey.

"I want to know now!" he insisted.

At that moment a knock sounded on the door. Audrey went to the screen and looked out. It was a delivery boy with a large box for me. I was in no condition to open it so Audrey untied the ribbon and lifted the lid. She took out a gorgeous orchid lei. The card was signed "Walton."

"So that's it," said Gil bitterly as he gazed at the lei.

"You don't understand. You probably never will," I sobbed.

139

"I can understand a gift like that. Whom are you going away with, Kimiko?" he asked.

"It doesn't matter, Gil. Take my word for it," said Audrey.

"You stay out of this!" He glared. He swung around to me. "Who is the man?"

"Walton Creet."

Gil had never heard of him. "Do you love him?"

"No. He knows I don't."

"Then why are you leaving with him?"

I burst into tears. I should have remained in Tokyo and taken my chances on remaining alive. I didn't belong in the West where emotions ruled the only profession I knew. My home was in the teeming islands of Japan where a geisha's way of life was understood and approved.

"You've got to leave, Gil. I mean it!" said Audrey. This time she would not be intimidated. She took him by the arm and pushed him toward the door.

"I can't let you go," he said brokenly.

"For your own good, and hers, you've got to. I'll explain it all to you later. If she stays on this island, she's sunk. Now please go. You'll see her again some day," said the Chinese girl. She gave him a kindly smile.

Gil looked at me as I sat on the edge of the couch sobbing.

"But—" He looked at Audrey helplessly.

"I promise she'll come back to you," she said. If she was lying, she couldn't help it. Something had to be done. "I've never gone back on my word yet."

She eased Gil through the door. Outside she again reminded him to see her the next time he was on Oahu. Gil walked away, his shoulders drooping.

Audrey was a big help in getting me calmed down when she came back inside. When the hysteria had left my eyes I looked around.

140

"Are you sure he's gone?" I asked tonelessly.

"Yes."

My eyes filled once more. Audrey watched me closely. "That's what you wanted, wasn't it?"

"Yes. You're right."

"Then snap out of it. You've got to finish packing."

It didn't matter much any longer. Mechanically I dropped things into the open suitcases. It was Audrey who finally did the packing for me. My new suit arrived and we began dressing.

George and Walton were coming to take us to dinner. From there we would go to the airport where George and Audrey would see us off. The Western-style suit was new to me and at first it did not seem to give comfort. When I was dressed, Audrey hung the orchid lei about my shoulders and stood back to look at me.

"By golly, you might make the movies at that," she laughed.

I only shrugged.

At six o'clock George and Walton arrived. The two men were already in a festive spirit. They carried my bags to the car and the four of us drove to one of the best restaurants at Waikiki. Audrey quickly got into the spirit of the occasion, but I had difficulty coming out of my dejection. I drank three cocktails before dinner and did my best to seem congenial. But my heart was still leaden as we drove to the airport that evening.

We turned off Kamahameha Highway onto the airport road. As the lights of the mid-Pacific terminal loomed before me, I had the feeling that a significant portion of my life was about to disappear forever. We checked in our luggage. The tickets were stamped. At eight o'clock we stood on the ramp waiting for the flight to be announced. Audrey took me aside.

141

"If any police show up, keep your face hidden somehow," she said softly.

I had forgotten about the Sandman and his threat. I glanced around fearfully, but all I saw were waiting passengers, bedecked in leis, surrounded by friends wishing them alohas and speedy returns to the Islands.

"I wish I were going with you," cried George. "I haven't been home in two years."

"All right, let's get on the plane with them," said Audrey.

It was during this exchange of pleasantries that the loud speaker blared. The flight was being called. I had no further time for regretting. It was time to go. Walton's hand pressed my arm. I glanced up at him and tried to smile.

"Good-bye, Kimiko. And come back some day," said Audrey with tears in her eyes.

I waved back at her. We moved with the crowd toward the plane. I hardly knew what I was doing as we mounted the stairs to be greeted by a pert, smiling hostess. Walton guided me to a seat. My racing brain had little time to think that this was the first air flight I had ever taken. Walton helped me fasten the safety belt.

"We're going to a world of happiness," said Walton, patting my knee.

"I—I hope so," I said, choking back my tears.

Suddenly the engines roared. I was too unhappy to be frightened. The great plane began to move. I was forced back against the cushions of the seat as it gathered momentum on the runway.

I glanced through the round porthole. The lights of Honolulu already were below. In that moment of confusion and despair, I doubted if I would ever see them again.

CHAPTER EIGHTEEN

We came down through the mists to a rain-drenched airport the next morning. I shivered in the chilling dampness as we left the plane. I looked about wonderingly for I had always had an avid curiosity about this vast, fabulous land, the United States. Before we changed to another plane I caught a glimpse of San Francisco, that enchanting city on the bay.

Again we were on our way, flying southward this time. And in less than two hours we landed at an airport, sunnier and more friendly than the first. Walton noticed the pensive expression on my face and smiled questioningly.

"How do you like California?"

"It seems quite lovely. Is this the way Illinois is?"

"Illinois?" he laughed. "What's that got to do with it?"

"I only wondered."

I moved off with him, thinking of Gil's homeland. A chauffeur awaited Walton and held open the door of a large limousine. As we rode into Los Angeles, Walton pointed out places of interest that I had never heard of. In time we traveled up a winding street in Beverly Hills and turned into a private drive that led to his home.

"Welcome, baby," said Walton. He grinned as he helped me out of the car.

I looked up at a large, rambling white house that was worth a fortune. Beyond the hedge was a bright, blue swimming pool. We crossed the patio and entered the house. Walton turned me over to a pretty French maid who led me to a suite of rooms on the second floor.

"I hope your stay here will be a pleasant one," said the maid as she began to unpack my luggage.

"Thank you." I noted the hint in the maid's words as to the temporary nature of the arrangement. All I hoped was that it lasted long enough for me to become acclimated to this new country.

"Walton found you in Hawaii undoubtedly, did he not?"

"Yes." I wondered if it were the custom for a maid to address her employer by his first name.

The girl gave a melodious laugh. "He loves foreign things. Two years ago he brought me here from Paris. I lived in these rooms for a while."

"I hope I am not intruding," I said quickly.

"Not at all. Others have been here. It only happened that I was adaptable to domestic service. His peccability no longer interests me."

The girl was so pleasantly indifferent about it that I had to smile. But it set me to thinking. Perhaps my time here was more limited than I had thought. I asked the maid's advice about clothes, and the former mistress immediately began to prove her goodwill. She told me many things I needed to know about Walton's likes and dislikes.

Later in the morning she returned with large boxes. When she opened them I stared in amazement. They contained Japanese kimonos, zori and obi. I looked at her in perplexity.

"Walton ordered them for you. He wants you to wear them," she explained.

"Had I known I would not have bought the suit I arrived in."

The maid laughed. "It's a whim of his. At noon he wants you to join him at the pool."

"In one of these?" I picked up a kimono. In Japan I had never seen one so expensive and gorgeous.

"No. It's for a swim. The kimonos are for other times."

Late that morning I put on swim trunks and a bra and went down. Walton was reclining comfortably in a deck chair with a drink in his hand. He waved me to a chair.

"I am told you want me to dress Japanese," I said.

He smiled. "Geisha, did I send you the right stuff? I called an importer who said he knew what you would need."

"They're lovely kimonos, Walton. I have never seen anything quite like them."

"And I'll bet you'll look lovelier than ever in them. Did Jeanne take care of, you all right?" he asked.

"Oh, the French maid. Yes. She was very kind," I assured him.

"She'll be at your service whenever you need anything. Tonight we go to a dinner party with some friends of mine. You'll knock their eyes out, if I'm any judge. They don't know what a real geisha is like," he chuckled. "Have a drink, Kimiko."

I accepted a highball. It was the beginning of endless drinking with him. He never seemed content without a drink in his hand. Later we enjoyed a swim and lunched at the side of the pool.

That evening, dressed in a kimono and my zori and obi, I went to the dinner party with Walton. There were a dozen other people present and they all looked at me curiously as Walton introduced me. The women regarded me closely but with reservation. The men beamed. I felt as if I were on display as a novelty.

145

Once I found myself visiting in the company of two men and a dazzling blonde. Suddenly the blonde turned to me.

"I didn't get to meet you when Walton made the introduction. What did you say your name was?"

"Kimiko," I replied, then added politely, "and yours?"

The blonde stiffened. She glared haughtily at me, then dragged one of the men off with her to get a drink. I stared after her in bewilderment. The man at my side laughed.

"Don't you know who she is?" he asked.

"No. I'm sorry. Was I supposed to?" I glanced up at him for enlightenment.

"That pan of Doreen's has shown from every motion picture screen and billboard in the country."

"I have seen no billboards and have been to picture shows only a half-dozen times in my life," I told him. "I'm sorry, I didn't know."

"What was that you said?" he asked, staring at me incredulously.

I gestured helplessly. Walton and Jeanne should have told me if I was expected to know such things. I didn't know it then, but my notoriety as Walton Creet's newest mistress was overshadowed by the insult I had handed a great motion picture star.

That evening was the first of a long succession of parties. When introducing me, Walton always made a point of the fact that I had been a geisha. It seemed to please him. In time I came to know the members of the charmed circle of film celebrities, but I never stood in awe for I never fully appreciated what they were famous for.

I felt unnecessarily conspicuous in a kimono at the parties, but Walton insisted that I wear one. I would have much preferred American dress on those occasions. And I believe that Walton's friends eventually grew bored with such an obvious display.

Perhaps it was this that caused Walton's first trace of displeasure with me. He did not understand it himself. He only knew that as we went to more and more places, I appeared to him as more and more commonplace.

His annoyance showed itself a couple of times when he had been drinking heavily. I found it more difficult to please him. During the days I spent many hours at the pool. Quite often, friends of Walton were there. I made myself as agreeable as possible with them but their interests were not mine and I found it hard to sustain conversation.

I had a feeling that my time with Walton was running out. A couple of other girls were competing for his attention and he brought them more often to his swimming pool. I felt no jealousy. I had to be available to him when he wanted me. I didn't know what else to do. One day Jeanne reported that another girl had spent the night in his bedroom.

"He seems to be quite interested in her," she said.

I must have appeared worried to her for she added, "You knew it would happen sooner or later."

"Of course. That isn't what concerns me," I said.

"No?" Jeanne lifted her eyebrows in surprise.

"I know so little about the United States. If he turns me out, I will need employment."

"What sort of work would you do?"

"I know only one kind." I waved significantly toward the bed.

Jeanne grinned. "Your problem is something like the one I faced. There are lots of call girls in Los Angeles, and the competition is fierce. There are too many amateurs on the loose. If you wish to be a lady of enjoyment, go elsewhere."

147

"But where? I know nothing about the country. I know little enough about Los Angeles."

During the six weeks I had lived with Walton, I had never gone away from the house by myself. All I knew of the city was what I had seen from this hilltop. At night I had driven with Walton to parties or to restaurants and the rides presented me with little more scenery than miles of neon and lighted display windows.

"Unless you particularly like Hollywood, I wouldn't stay here if I were you," Jeanne suggested.

"Where should I go?"

"San Francisco, perhaps. There are a lot of Oriental people there. You may be better off among those who understand you."

The days grew more monotonous as Walton paid less and less attention to me. I rarely went out with him at night. He went out alone to meet other girls. Sometimes he returned drunk and visited my rooms. Once he brought home a friend and turned him over to me for the remainder of the night. The friend returned, uninvited, a week later and was there when Walton arrived home.

"What the hell is going on here?" he demanded.

The man left in a hurry. I could not understand Walton's rage. The man had visited me before at Walton's request.

"I want you out of here in an hour!" he stormed, slapping me viciously across the face.

He flung some bills at me and left in a fit of anger. I calmed myself and gathered the money. There were three-one-hundred dollar bills, a fifty and half a dozen twenties. It was a relief to know that I was through with Walton Creet. My position had been too uncertain for the past two weeks. I began the melancholy task of packing my things.

"What happened?" asked Jeanne hurrying in.

I explained briefly.

"I'm sorry, Kimiko."

"Don't be, for I'm not. My only worry is getting myself established elsewhere."

I took Jeanne's advice and bought a bus ticket to San Francisco, arriving the next day. The sun was bright and the air was tangy; there was a new spring in my step. I found a cheap hotel with an ancient marble lobby on Clay Street. When the bellboy left me alone in the room, I sat down and let the tears come. I felt better after an hour of rest.

After dinner in a dimly lighted restaurant across the street, I took a long walk. Directions meant nothing to me. I was not frightened when I discovered that I was hopelessly lost. I delighted in watching the little cable cars and looking into the windows at the heavily made clothing. I pulled the collar of my coat up closer around my neck against the chill of the evening and moved on. In time and to my surprise I found myself surrounded by Chinese shops. Unknowingly I had walked along Grant Street to Chinatown.

I entered a shop and an old Chinese man appeared from behind a curtain in the rear. He looked me over inscrutably.

"I am a stranger in this city and in the morning I wish to seek employment. Would you be so kind as to make a suggestion?" I asked.

"What work do you seek?"

"I am a geisha."

"There is no work for you here." He shook his head and frowned.

"No houses?"

"No."

I sensed that he had little sympathy for a Japanese geisha, but I persisted. I had to talk with someone.

149

"What other sort of work would be open to a girl?"

"The department stores hire clerks all the time. Go there. Trying will do no harm. There is always the other occupation to turn to," he shrugged.

I thanked him and left the shop. The more I considered his suggestion, the better I liked it. I didn't know if I could make the grade, but, as he had said, I could try. I walked three blocks, feeling strangely at home in this Oriental section of the city. But in time I grew tired and asked directions to my hotel. I discovered that it was only two blocks away.

The next morning I was hired for the first legitimate job I'd ever had. I was astounded when the man in the employment office of a store on Market Street talked with me, then announced that I could go to work at once if I cared to.

"You are very kind," I told him softly.

He glanced at me quickly, his eyes alert. Then he smiled. "What makes you say that?"

"I didn't know it was possible to obtain employment so easily."

"It isn't for every girl. You're good-looking. We can use you on our main floor. It helps drag in men customers."

I was taken downstairs and introduced to the woman in charge of the hosiery department. I spent that morning learning the stock and how to make out sales slips. In the afternoon I waited on customers and was delighted with my success when the day was over at five o'clock. That night as I went to sleep in my hotel room I wondered if it was possible that I could begin a life of respectability.

I received more satisfaction out of that first week's work than I had imagined possible. It was tiring at first, but I got over that after a couple of days. On Saturday night I was handed a pay envelope which I tucked safely in my purse and carried to the hotel room. As I counted my earnings, the smile vanished from my face. I looked in the envelope to see if I had gotten it all out. I counted the money again.

My earnings didn't equal my hotel bill for the week, to say nothing of my food. I was stunned. This would never do. At this rate, the money I had salvaged from Walton would soon be gone. Something had to be done quickly. It didn't take long for me to realize what I had to do.

In the lobby later that evening I got the bell captain aside and asked what arrangements I could make for entertaining men in my room.

"I've been wondering about you," he smirked. "What you want can be arranged but I get girls in here from a syndicate. You've got to work through them. We'll both get in trouble if you don't."

"Can you put me in touch with the right people?"

He nodded. "There's a girl who comes around to make arrangements. Go to your room and wait. I'll have her come up to talk with you."

I went to my room. I smoked several cigarettes as I waited. That pay envelope from the department store had been a blow. I wondered how the other girls who clerked there made out. They couldn't live on those wages. Perhaps they too supplemented their incomes. It never occurred to me to live somewhere other than a hotel. Where else was there? Presently there was a knock at my door. I opened it and a large girl with blonde hair and hard eyes walked in.

I gazed at her in bewilderment. Vague recollections flitted through my mind. Then all at once, recognition leaped into my eyes. It was Helen Gray, the girl who had hated me so at Mrs. Reisner's.

"What are you doing in San Francisco?" said Helen thinly when she recognized me.

"I—I'm looking for work."

"Did they kick you out of the islands?" A contemptuous smile played around Helen's mouth.

"No. I left of my own accord. I've been living in Los Angeles." I felt sick. If this was the girl I had to make a deal with, I was ruined.

"So now you want to get in on things here, eh? This is good. It really is. Just what do you suppose your chances are of making a living?" asked Helen acidly.

"Are you the one the bell captain said I would have to talk with?"

"I sure am. And you're never going to work in this town. I can promise that right now. If you even look cross-eyed at a man I'll send some goons to work you over. When they finish with a girl no man wants her ever again. I'd just love to see them giving you the business."

"I'm sorry I bothered you, Helen." I saw no point in talking with her further.

"Not so fast, my friend. I have a score to settle with you," said Helen, her voice thin and menacing. "I've got influence in this town and when I say a girl is no good, my friends take my word for it. I don't even want you in the same town with me. Do you understand what I mean?"

"But if I don't have men up to my room—" I began.

"That makes no difference. I'll check around in a few days. If you're still here you'll have some visitors who'll give you a good time. A real good time," Helen warned.

All at once she laughed at me. She walked to the door. With a final sneer, she disappeared into the hotel corridor.

I sat down limply on the bed. Helen Gray meant what she had said. If I remained in San Francisco, the girl would get me. I would walk in fear every moment of the time. But where to go now? Of all the people

152

in this great, gray city of sunlight and steep hills, I knew only one. And she hated me more than anyone else in the world. Frantic desperation began racing through my brain.

CHAPTER NINETEEN

All I could think of was getting home. I would rather risk the jeopardy on my life than continue the uncertainty of existence in places and among people I could not understand. I was filled with nostalgia for my homeland. I wanted to go back to Japan. But crossing the Pacific with my limited funds would be a problem.

The next afternoon I made fruitless inquiries of shipping firms along the Embarcadero. I was sitting dejectedly in a seamen's restaurant on Bryant Street under the Bay Bridge, sipping a cup of coffee and a stranger sat down at my table. I was deep in thought and did not notice him at first.

"I know you from somewhere, girlie," he said.

I looked up. He was an older man, possibly fifty-five. His hair was white and his eyes were a watery blue. He drank half of his coffee, then looked at me again.

"I know. You came on the _Harrison-Jay_ with us once from Hakodate. You had a deal of some sort with Captain Mert Hagan as I recall."

The _Harrison-Jay_ was the ship I had sailed on to Hawaii. I studied the man a moment and gradually his face emerged in my memory.

"You were the mate on that ship!" I exclaimed.

"That's right."

154

We exchanged pleasantries. As I sat with him an idea suddenly came to my mind.

"Is the *Harrison-Jay* in San Francisco? Is Captain Hagan here?" If he were, I could make a deal with him. I would do anything if he would take me back to Japan.

The man shook his head. "I left them in Honolulu last week. Came on here by ship to find work. I'm tired of the sea."

The hope that had flared in me quickly died down. I finished my coffee and was about to get up when another possibility came to mind. It was so forlorn that I very nearly discarded it.

"Is there a chance that the *Harrison-Jay* is still in Honolulu?" I asked.

"Yep. She's still there, as far as I know. Probably tied up at Sand Island for some repair work on the rudder. We had trouble with it the last trip."

"Would it still be there for the next day or so?" I cried with sudden excitement.

"Sure it would. It'll take a couple of days to load after the repairs are made."

"Where is it going from Honolulu?"

"Nagasaki, I think," said the man.

"Thank you so very much!"

I arose and hurried out. I got a taxi and told the driver to take me to the airline office as soon as possible. On the way I did some calculation in my mind. As nearly as I could figure, I had just about enough money to get me to Honolulu by plane. If the *Harrison-Jay* was still there I would make arrangements with the Captain for my passage to Japan.

Thirty minutes later I was told I could have a reservation on the night plane leaving for Hawaii. That afternoon I checked out of the hotel and found transportation to the International Airport. Everything was

155

working out. I hoped that Helen Gray was satisfied. I was getting out of town . . . out of the country. I felt better than I had in weeks and enjoyed the dinner that I ate at the airport.

When the flight was called for the Honolulu-bound plane I was the first one in line to get aboard.

During the long, dark flight across two thousand miles of ocean, I considered the problem of the police and the Sandman. Surely, after all this time, they would have forgotten about me. I could find sanctuary at the apartment with Audrey until my arrangements with Captain Hagan were complete. In time I dropped off to sleep in the reclining chair of the plane.

When I awoke in the sunlight of early morning, the plane was turning on Diamond Head. It seemed to me as if I was coming home. After landing, I went directly by taxi to Audrey's apartment at Waikiki.

"My gosh! I'm seeing things!" Audrey exclaimed when I walked in at ten o'clock that morning.

"Hello, Audrey."

There was so much the Chinese girl wanted to know that it took me a whole hour to relate what had happened to me in America. When I finally got caught up, I went to the telephone and called the Aloha Tower. From the Port Authority's office I learned that the *Harrison-Jay* had not yet sailed. Luck was indeed with me.

"Now if I can just locate Captain Hagan," I said.

"Why go to Nagasaki? Hilo would be the place for you," Audrey smiled.

"Have you seen Gil?"

"I have. Several times," said Audrey promptly. "And he's still in love with you, do you know it?"

My eyes softened. For a moment my heart filled with yearning for him. Then quickly I put such thoughts aside. That was no good, feeling like that all over

156

again. My resolve stiffened. I grabbed up my purse.

"I've got to go into Honolulu," I said. "Mind if I leave my things here? And I might even be needing to sleep here tonight if I may."

"Glad to have you," said Audrey.

A peculiar expression crossed her face. Her eyes narrowed. It did not impress me as particularly significant at that instant. I was in too much of a hurry to find Captain Hagan.

It took me the better part of the afternoon to locate him. And it took me another hour to talk him into giving me passage on his ship. I promised to pay him twice over for his trouble.

"All right," he finally agreed. "You catch the harbor launch at eleven o'clock tonight. It'll bring you to the *Harrison-Jay*. We're sailing shortly after midnight. If you're not there, you're out of luck, Kimiko."

"I'll be there." Tears of gratitude filled my eyes.

I returned to the apartment at six. Audrey had prepared dinner in anticipation of my return. But her face fell when I said that I was to board the harbor launch at eleven o'clock that night.

Audrey had no date that night. She had pulled on her short mandarin jacket and after dinner we chatted over our coffee and cigarettes. Audrey reminded me that I was crazy for going back to Japan. She said there was a much greater future for me here in Hawaii.

"Crazy or not, I'm going."

I glanced at the clock. It was nearly ten-thirty. I had just enough time to change into an older dress that would look more appropriate for boarding the *Harrison-Jay*. I opened a suitcase.

"What time does the harbor launch shove off?" asked Audrey.

"At eleven sharp. Do you mind calling a taxi for me?"

I took off my dress. I laid it on the couch and bent

over to fold it for packing in the suitcase in place of the older one I was going to put on.

Audrey got out of her chair. But instead of going to the telephone she walked over and stood behind me. I glanced over my shoulder to see what she was doing.

Suddenly she grabbed hold of me. The room spun and before I knew what had happened I was lying on my back. I looked up in startled wonder as Audrey straddled my belly.

"Why are you doing this?" I asked.

"Do you really want to go to Japan?"

"Of course. And I've got to hurry. Get off."

An insolent smile crossed Audrey's mouth as she sat on me. Slowly she shook her head. I wondered if she had taken leave of her senses. There was no reason for such peculiar behavior. I frowned.

"Let me up!"

"You're not going on that ship tonight," she said.

"Who are you to say I can't?"

"Isn't that a silly question? Look at the position you're in."

Her taunts aroused my resentment. It turned to anger when she made no move to let me up. I rolled my head so I could see the clock. Time was running out.

I made a sudden frenzied effort to get free. Audrey grabbed my wrists and pinned them down. I tried to roll over but was hopelessly clasped between her legs. Presently I lay panting. In my exhaustion I knew I could never force her off.

"You don't know what you're doing," I sobbed.

"A certain man made me promise not to let you get away if you ever showed up again."

I stared up at her incredulously. The Sandman! She was going to turn me over to him. No doubt she'd collect a fee for her trouble. All at once this girl's pretended friendship was explained. If she couldn't collect

158

money from me as her roommate, she'd collect another way.

In a burst of anger I cursed her treachery, first in English, then Japanese. She gave a scornful laugh. I saw the clock again. It was already after eleven.

"I hope you're satisfied," I said bitterly.

"Not yet."

"But you've already caused me to miss the harbor launch."

"The ship doesn't sail until after midnight. Didn't you say that?" Audrey smiled at my torment.

I lay outstretched and helpless. I had thought of trying some way to get to the ship in spite of having missed the launch. But with this girl keeping me prisoner, I didn't have a chance. I gave up in despair.

A knock came at the door around midnight. Audrey got up to answer it. I was so tired and heartsick that I could not move. Nothing mattered at all. I was fated from the beginning to a life beyond my control. I heard Audrey's voice.

"I had a heck of a time keeping her for you, but there she is. The rest is up to you, my friend."

"Your message came just in time. I caught the last plane from Hilo. Thanks so very much, Audrey."

Every nerve in my body was jolted by that voice. I raised up. Then, without looking around, I thought it could not be true. It was one more evil delusion, like my misplaced trust in Audrey Ching. I could hardly believe my eyes as Gil appeared at my side an instant later.

"I knew you'd come back, Kimiko. And I want you more than ever," he said, gathering me to him.

I gazed at him as if witnessing a miracle. The pressure of his arms was real. Faith suddenly unshackled my heart and a burst of hope swept the desolate gloom from my mind. At last I saw the wonderful meaning of

159

our love. It transcended all barriers. I could not avoid its joyous fulfillment. I no longer wanted to. My lips moved toward his.

"I'll never leave you again, Gil. Never!" I cried as happiness flooded through me.

I have kept that promise ever since, as Mrs. Gil Dawson of Hilo, Hawaii—once a geisha of Tokyo, Japan.

THE END

Lightning Source UK Ltd.
Milton Keynes UK
UKOW06f1934140616

276320UK00008B/166/P